Balancing Your
Core Belief System
A Positive Process
John Bligh Nutting

The Growing Awareness Series - Amazon Kindle Edition

Balancing your core belief system : a positive process / John Bligh Nutting (author).

Date of Publication - March 2020 Sold by: Amazon Digital Services LLC

ASIN: B07HLNFXMP

National Library of Australia - Publication Data 2018, English, Book edition: CBal-1

Bookmark: https://trove.nla.gov.au/version/258232379 - Edition - First.

Published Bald Hills, QLD : Growing Awareness, 2018. Language English

Edition details

Title: Balancing your core belief system : a positive process / John Bligh Nutting (author). Edition First.Kindle

Published Bald Hills, QLD : Growing Awareness, 2018.

Content Types text Series CBal ; CBal-1

Subjects - Self-help & personal development. Mind, body, spirit. Self-esteem. Interpersonal Relations. Self Actualisation (Psychology). Life skills. Australian Target Audience: General

Summary

Core beliefs were created in childhood to help us survive by believing something negative about ourselves that was not really true. That belief helped us fit in with our family and make sense of what we were experiencing. Back then we needed to do that far more than we needed to feel good about ourselves. But even after we become adults, those old unbalanced core beliefs don't go away. They continue to exert an incredibly powerful but negative influence over our life. Core Beliefs are different from other kinds of beliefs, and because they are part of your unconscious and well hidden, you won't be aware of them. This book shows you how to detect, identify and then balance your old negative core belief with a new positive belief.

Notes

Language English

ISBN 9780975700914

Libraries Australia ID 64275003

Amazon

Contributed by Libraries Australia

Published in Australia by Growing Awareness Pty Ltd
PO Box 133
Bald Hills Q 4036

Cell / Mobile +61 414 57 00 16

E-mail: *bligh4@growingaware.com*

NATIONAL LIBRARY OF AUSTRALIA

A catalogue record for this book is available from the National Library of Australia

Author and Publisher's Waiver

The author and publishers of this book do not dispense or recommend medical or psychiatric advice, nor prescribe the use of any technique as a form of treatment for any diagnosable medical or psychiatric conditions. Any such action should only be taken either directly or indirectly on the advice of your physician or a qualified therapist.

The intent of the author and publisher of this book is only to offer information and self awareness exercises of a general nature to help you in your search for love, growth, freedom, understanding and emotional well-being.

In the event that you choose to use any of the information in this book or complete any of the personal activity sheets for yourself, you are choosing or prescribing such activities for yourself, which is your personal right, but the author and publisher assume no responsibility for your actions nor any outcomes claimed to be connected with what are your own personal choices.

The Growing Awareness Series - The Key to Balancing Your Life

Book CBal-1

Balancing Your Core Belief System

It's a Positive Process

Once you start seeing your own old or negative core beliefs more clearly you can then balance them with new positive ones. You will find yourself making powerful, positive changes in your life, the changes you have always wanted to make, the changes that make a real difference.

Core belief balancing also helps people choose when they want to make their changes and how and where they want to make them.

That is wonderfully self-empowering.

Getting to know and understand about your core beliefs, your over-reaction patterns, compensating skills, core issue and how to balance them, are important steps that most people need to take before they can continue with their work of Growing and Climbing, Self Empowerment and Flying Free.

- ***make things happen, get things done, the way you want, when and how you want***
- ***make powerful, positive changes in your life, the changes you have always wanted to make, the changes that make a real difference.***
- ***increase your self confidence as you grow your Personal Power***
- ***using your self determination skills, your power to choose, to decide, to determine who you are and what you will do with your life.***
- ***discover the person you really are - becoming the true you and realise your potential for living***
- ***overcome blockages that limit your right to be a self-empowered, authentic, grown-up individual***
- ***find more love, freedom, success and real joy in your life***
- ***grow and enrich your relationships - create new intimacy, new and deeper bonding with a partner, friends, family***
- ***self-heal your deepest emotional pain and sorrow***

John Bligh Nutting

SELF-AWARENESS → SELF -EMPOWERMENT → POWER TO CHANGE MY LIFE → SELF-HEALING

About the Author

John Bligh Nutting

B.A.(Psych)

Qualified lecturer, psychotherapist and facilitator, with over thirty five years' experience. BA. Degree with double major in Psychology (University of Queensland 1974)

Now retired - Past Memberships included :
MQCA (Clinical) (Retired) Australian Register of Counsellors and Psychotherapists - ARCAP; National Australian Register - Psychotherapists and Counsellors Federation Australia (PACFA) (Retired) ; State Register - Clinical Counsellor - (Retired) Queensland Counsellors Association (QCA) 230-80156; Past Member, International Society for the Study of Trauma and Dissociation Professional Member, Adults Surviving Child abuse (ASCA)

Specialist fields include core belief and inner self training, developing functional grown up and key life abilities, open communication and intimacy; overcoming blockages (sexual, emotional and negativity), self-esteem, boundary growth, repetitive self-defeating patterns, codependency and addictions.

Studies in relationship and personal growth include working and training with Dr. Hal Stone and Dr. Sidra Stone in Australia and the USA and three weeks' internship at The Meadows in Arizona (with Pia and Pat Mellody).

He worked as a facilitator-therapist with Dr. John Bradshaw in Brisbane and Sydney, during Dr. Bradshaw's 1994 Australian tour.

He also lectured at the Australian College of Natural Medicine, and conducted voice dialogue training seminars for Lifeline and other organisations, focusing on relationship, power and control issues and their effect on people at work and in relationships. In 1995 in the USA, he completed the Harville Hendrix course 'Getting the Love You Want'. In 1997 he trained with gifted Russian energy teacher Sergei Gorsky.

John is the author of the Australian best seller *'The Business of Communicating'* (McGraw-Hill) which has sold over 100,000 copies. His next book *'Growing Awareness'* published in 2000 was a set text for students at the Australian College of Natural Medicine.

His latest works in the 'Growing Awareness' series are already published on the internet and will be available later this year in print.

His training and counselling methods have been developed from the work of all the above teachers with additional specialist training, including Post Induction Therapy training (South Pacific Hospital NSW 1996) and accredited EMDR training in Brisbane in 1997.

His training programs on Balancing Core Beliefs, Emotional Age Awareness and the Inner Matriarch and Inner Patriarch are gaining growing international recognition. His Core Belief work has been translated into German.

John runs training groups on Emotional Age Awareness, Core Belief Balancing; Inner Child and Self Empowerment in Brisbane and on the Queensland North Coast and Gold Coast as well as in other Australian states. He also conducts personal one-to-one voice dialogue training, inner child work and counselling throughout the world, by phone and over the internet.

For the latest news on John's Core Belief, Self empowerment, Inner child training and other Growing Awareness groups please check any of John's websites :

www.core-beliefs-balance.com
www.realme1.com
www.love-your-inner-child.com
www.voice-dialogue-inner-self-awareness.com
www.growing-aware.com.au

E-mail:

bligh4@growingaware.com

Phone:

John can be contacted on
Cell phone +61.414 570 016 (international)
Cell or mobile phone 0414 570 016 (in Australia)

Table of Contents

Balancing Your Core Belief System

Even Understanding an old Negative Core Belief is a Positive Process

Core Belief work is NOT Therapy.
It cannot 'heal' nor 'cure' nor 'fix'

Self awareness, self empowerment and core belief balancing are powerful processes.
But they are NOT therapy and must never be presented as if they are therapeutic in nature or intention. They are in no way suggested as a cure nor treatment for any diagnosable condition, whether physical or psychological in nature.
They may however compliment other treatments by helping develop a more positive outlook about one's self, one's body, self-esteem and autherntic vulnerability. If the diagnosable condition is partly related to non-physical or ACE issues the chances of improvement are then likely to increase.

Acknowledgement - Nikki Nemerouf creator of the Core Paradigm and the Gifts concept

This all started late in 1997 when I trained with Nikki Nemerouf on what was then a radical new approach to the problems people so often experienced with out-of-control behaviour patterns, over-reactions that just seemed to switch on automatically. Nikki noticed that even though these reactions were repeatedly triggered by the same words or events, many people seemed unable to do anything about the connection between trigger events and their over reactions.

"Money, time, relationships, professional skills, family, everything has been reorganised so that it can be better used to distance me from my pain, my vulnerability and my fear of my negative beliefs getting any worse than they already are.
In doing so I also distance myself from the love or power or freedom or happiness or wealth or health or safety or whatever I am desperately seeking"
(Nikki Nemerouf)

He said it was as though they had been automatically "hot wired" to something that troubled them, deep inside.

However, once they identified their hidden core belief, they were then able to switch from, as he put it, *"operating automatically to living authentically"*. But things didn't stop there. Somehow, identifying and naming a core belief also unlocked a whole range of other positive energies. Many people later described what happened as a *"life altering experience."* Careers, relationships, finances, family, even health all started to improve.

It seemed as though just one negative belief had been holding them back, not just with its automatic triggered reactions but in many other ways as well.

That understanding made so much sense to me and as soon as I identified my own so very well hidden core belief my own life started to get better, a lot better.

I thanked Nikki back then and enquired why he hadn't put this in a book. He said he just hadn't got round to it. As far as I know, the last time I talked to him a few years ago he still hadn't.

Can you sense the paradox of a protection system that is trying to get someone else to help ease your hurting at the same time as it is trying to hide that pain from them!
Nikki Nemerouf

He still prefers to present his work live, as a high level coach working with executive training groups in the USA. Here's his link:
www.slideshare.net/nikkinemerouf/starquest-llc

But back then Nikki was also kind enough to give me permission to write about his work, adapt it and include it in a text book I was about to publish "Growing Awareness" as long as I acknowledged him as the originator.

That's how early in 1998, I became the first author in the world to publish details of his Core Belief Paradigm and describe ways to deal with it.

My website *www.core-beliefs-balance.com* followed in 1999 and attracted over 1,000 hits in its first month on line. There wasn't much about core beliefs on the web back then.

On the website and in my book, I described easy ways to identify the hidden Core beliefs behind so many personal and professional barriers, and the tools to over come them. People who do that then go on to embrace a deeper sense of change that as Nikki says *"allows them to transform their lives and relationships"*.

I've rewritten the story several times but you'll notice throughout the pages of every edition I continue to acknowledge Nikki's insight and wisdom and the gratitude we owe to him for sharing his pioneering work with Core Beliefs.

I've added my own training on Emotional Age, Self Awareness, Self empowerment, and of course Balancing opposite beliefs with Emotional Gym.

Author's note - Acknowledgements

I gratefully acknowledge the valuable guidance, support and understandings I continue to receive as I write my books.

I acknowledge the valuable understanding I gained from author Pia Mellody, Pat Mellody and the brilliant team of therapists at "The Meadows" in Wickenberg Arizona USA where I trained in the early 1990s as an intern.

The many important lessons about love, life, self awareness and dependency that I learned there made a major contribution towards my understanding and identification of inner child issues. I also thank Pat and Pia for their kind permission for me to quote from their work.

I acknowledge the pioneering developments on the psychology of the inner selves by Dr. Hal Stone and Dr. Sidra Stone. Their contribution to my understanding of self-awareness and energy balancing cannot be underestimated. Their work has changed my life.

As a trained Voice Dialogue facilitator, I acknowledge their teachings on which the energy balancing process in these books is based. You'll notice my reference to self awareness, voice dialogue and energy balancing throughout the pages of each and every one of my books.

I cannot stress too strongly what Hal and Sidra Stone have taught the World, that inner self work (and therefore inner child work) can succeed only if it embraces these essential principles:

1. Our personality is comprised of many different parts. The most obvious ones we can describe as our sub-personalities or inner selves, or a dozen other similar names. Whatever we call them they are there all the time helping protect us and get us through the day.

2. The easiest and most authentic way to develop grown up self awareness, is by dialoguing with our inner sub-personalities, our inner children, or other inner protectors or as Hal and Sidra describe them, our inner selves.

3. This amazingly straight forward kind of dialogue or Voice Dialogue as it is generally known, is one of the most useful skills (often the critical success factor) in clarifying, core belief and inner child issues. I have found that dialoguing with the younger parts that are often so hard at work in each of us, is one of the most useful skills in clarifying, balancing and transforming any problem.

4. Adding emotional age awareness to our understanding of each sub-personality helps with balancing and leads to more positive outcomes. Balancing the younger parts of your personality and their emotional energies with their opposite but more grown up twins is a very effective way of improving life.

I cannot forget the earlier lessons from pioneer Eric Berne *"I'm OK, You're OK" (1969)* Berne introduced the idea of Transactional Analysis or TA. It is still as much a part of my work today as it was then. Nor have I forgotten the gifts from my Univertsity of Queensland lecturers who got me started in the 1970s, notably Bob Dick, John Damm and Elsie Harwood.

So many of the ideas in this book are based on the original work and the training I have undertaken with each of these true masters but I emphasise that my books do not follow precisely the models as taught by any of these outstanding teachers.

I have introduced some alternate concepts, in particular those based on the work of Dr. Jeffery Young, Earl Cass, Nikki Nemerouf and Sergei Gorsky who each added further understandings.

I thank Dr. John Falcon for his guidance, his valuable additions and most of all for introducing me to Core Belief balancing. That too changed my life.

I thank my son Anthony, now a Clinical Psychologist, my daughter Justine for her exceptional editing and design skills, (she helped me write this book) and my daughter Melinda for her lifelong support and her wisdom, my long term friend and illustrator Carol Scott; International Voice Dialogue trainer Martha Lou Woolf and the many other people who have helped me with their support and suggestions and for permitting me to include extracts from their own work in my books.

With appreciation - John Nutting

Brisbane Queensland Australia

March 2020

Comments - Reviews - Feedback

Thank you for our first couple of Zoom sessions. Your warm sense of humor and uncanny ability to see my core issue with compassion made me feel safe and confident. Moreover, I feel remarkably optimistic about my future because you are helping me to identify and heal my core wounds with a series of clear and precise exercises. The great Sufi poet Rumi once said, "Let yourself be silently drawn by the stronger pull of what you really love." Well- for the first time in my adult life I can honestly say that I am feeling that pull, and it's getting stronger everyday!

-KR, New York City

****

It's probably no surprise, but big changes going on here - much more positive, confident, and relaxed, and much less powerless as a result. A number of therapists had not been unable to make a dent in this powerlessness, so Core Belief Balancing is a huge step forward for me in terms of quality of life and hope for the future.

Based on our first Skype session I've been able to identify and tackle another belief on my own as well - "I am flawed/incompetent/a failure(?) because I can't perform." That's why I've been coaching and advising others, and why I don't like being seen/exposed in group situations where I can't control the outcome.

Also the source of my anxiety on turbulent planes (the cabin crew can't perform) or roller coasters (the machine can't perform). I haven't balanced this properly yet and might need your help. However, it's clear that there's really only one thing I definitely can't perform - miracles!

Can we book in another session for next week, either late morning or early afternoon to progress and go over whatever comes up between now and then?

TM - Macclesfield Cheshire UK

****

Thank you for our first short Skype session. It has helped give me greater perspective on myself and the situation at large. I will contact you next week for a longer session.

RR - Berkley - California

****

Just found your website today. Your insightful explanation of Negative Core Belief issues is already helping me to change some of the things that are happening in my life. I'd love a copy of your book and a chance to talk on Skype

Sunshine - Denver USA

****

I have had so much experience with Gestalt, TA and other self-awareness processes and modalities. None of them helped much with my problems. Since I started Core Belief Balancing in just a few weeks this has changed for me.

Gillian – Brighton - Queensland Australia

****

This is something I have been looking for, for ages. The straightforward discussion and examples make understanding and using core belief balancing so easy. It is working for me already. Please can I book another session.

FD - California USA

****

With Skype or even better with Zoom I am now able to work with you using the highly successful EMDR (Eye Movement Desensitising and Reprocessing) system, once you have installed the EMDR app on your iPhone or Android unit.
Ask me for the link

Free Web Workshops and Webinars

This year I plan to run regular interactive web-wokshops or webinars on Skype, Zoom and similar group conference platforms. These will be free to all purchasers of my books.

You will be able to ask me questions, share experiences, offer your own ideas on the work you are doing. There will be a special section for readers who have run into problems.

They will all be free. All you need to do now is register your name and e-mail address, country and time zone and I will contact you with news of the first session.

Introduction

Core Beliefs 101

Core beliefs can carry negative energy but they are not "bad." They were created in childhood to help us survive by believing something about ourselves that was not really true. But it was a useful belief because it helped us fit in with our family environment and make sense of what we were experiencing. And we needed to do that back then, far more than we needed to feel good about ourselves.

Old unbalanced core beliefs can continue to exert an incredibly powerful influence over our life. But because they are well hidden we can't see this.

Core Beliefs are Unconscious

These old beliefs are different from other kinds of beliefs, and because they are part of our unconscious we won't be aware of them.

A core belief is an energy state more than a thought. It's stored in your body as well as your unconscious mind.

No matter how hard people try by thinking consciously, rationally or analytically about it they just don't seem to be able to work out what their core belief might be or what it's doing,

What you can notice are some obvious signs such as repetitive out-of-control behaviour patterns, over-reactions that switch on automatically.

Even though these reactions are repeatedly triggered by the same words or events, so often people seem unable to change the connection between the trigger event and their "automatic" over reaction.

It's as though they have been automatically "hot wired" to something **that troubled them, deep inside.**

All kinds of problems

Being hot wired can lead to all kinds of problems in people's lives, damaged careers, wrecked relationships and reduced self-esteem at the same time as a reduction in your personal wealth and health suffers too.

A life altering experience

However, once a hidden core belief is identified and named, people can switch from *"operating automatically to living authentically" (Nemerouf*).

Improvements don't stop there. Identifying a core belief unlocks a whole range of other positive energies inside us. Many people later describe what happens then as a *"life altering experience."*

Careers, relationships, finances, family even health all start to improve too.

It seems as though that old negative belief had been holding them back, not just with automatic triggered reactions but in many other ways as well.

Balancing is the next step

Once people start seeing their own old or negative core beliefs more clearly they can balance the old one with a new positive one. They find themselves making powerful, positive changes in their life, the changes they have always wanted to make, the changes that make a real difference for them.

Core belief balancing also helps people choose when they want to make their changes and how and where they want to make them.

That is wonderfully self-empowering.

Discovering and then balancing my own core beliefs (twenty years ago) has helped me make so many positive changes in my life. These were changes that I wanted so much but somehow I just could not seem to make them happen until then.

The understanding made so much sense to me' As soon as I identified my own so very well hidden core belief and could see the harm my triggered over-reactions were doing to me, my life started to get better, a lot better.

The results have been so wonderful and so positive I wanted to share the whole story. Today thanks to the Internet and Amazon I am now able to share that story and the balancing process with people around the World.

Let's start - once you understand Core Beliefs then you can Discover yours, even though it's hidden

Part One - What is an Unbalanced Core Belief?

The old unbalanced core beliefs you and I are looking for here are well hidden. They are part of our unconscious so at the start you won't be aware of them.

Are you troubled (sometimes) deep inside by unspoken thoughts or feelings that go something like this:

"I am not good enough ."

"I am unlovable."

"I don't deserve to be happy."

"I have no value ."

"I am all wrong ."

"I don't belong . "

Sometimes rather than words they're just a feeling about who you are, or who you are not:

"I am a failure."

"I am a mistake"

"I am just not enough"

"I am worthless / inadequate"

If this happens for you (sometimes) you are not alone. Most people have thoughts like this but for many people what started out as just a background belief gradually becomes stroger and stronger.

There are at least eleven different groups of core belief patterns (the patterns listed in the box). Then within those eleven are probably over three hundred individual unbalanced Core beliefs.

To balance your own specific core belief with a positive one you need first to discover what your own specific "because I .." is about and name it.

Examples of core belief *"because I ..."* thoughts and feelings:

... because I am unlovable

... because I am powerless / worthless

... because I am damaged / broken /

... because I am defective, imperfect,

... because I am incompetent

... because I always lose

... because I am unseen / invisible / unheard

... because I don't count.

... because I don't fit in

... because I don't know how to

... because I am not safe

.. because I don't know,

... because I am always wrong

Yours will not be the same as the core beliefs held by people around you.

Those last statements are getting closer to the core of the belief. Today, not one of those statements is true or an accurate description of the person you really are, but telling you this, at this stage won't help much.

It can take over parts of our lives.

Often, around age 30 or 40 a negative belief starts to take control of your life. It sets up more and more blocks and it gets harder to control. Careers,

Unbalanced Negative core beliefs - general patterns

Unbalanced negative beliefs can be very different from person to person. Some are quite unique. Most core beliefs however are connected in a broad way with a sense of having no power, no self worth or not being good enough:

Old Core Belief Patterns	Core Issues
1. Not good enough (I am not safe)	**Security** Safety
2. Not good enough (I don't belong)	Belonging, Nurture **Self** care
3. Not good enough (I have no value, I am worthless)	**Self** worth
4. Not good enough (I am powerless, I have no value)	**Strength, Success,** Power Control
5. Not good enough (I am wrong, I am unsure)	Reality; Reason **Sanity**, Knowing
6. Not good enough (My life is out of balance)	Balance Moderation
7. Not good enough (I don't exist; I am nothing)	Identity; **Self**, Recognition
8. Not good enough (I am not real)	**Self** awareness, **Sanity**
9. Not good enough (I am unlovable; left out; unwanted)	Love, Loved and Loving
10. Not good enough (I am defective)	Health; Self healing, **Strength**
11. Not good enough (I am not whole I have lost my spirit)	Wholeness; **Spirit**

relationships and other important parts of your life all start to go downhill.

A Core Belief is Unconscious

It's unconscious but instead of slowing it down that makes it even stronger and of course it's harder to see what it's doing inside us. You can't deal with unconscious issues using logic or reasoning.

To discover your own old core belief, instead you work like an Inner Detective, looking at eight special clues or pointers and put the results together to 'identify the villain,' or in your case, name that hidden core belief that's been giving you so much trouble.

As soon as you name it, it starts to lose its power.

It's not unconscious any longer and you can keep an eye on it. After naming yours, Core Belief Balancing is the next step. It's not therapy, just basic energy balancing, a skill you already have.

Thousands of people around the World over the past 20 years have followed this easy and positive process and found how well it worked for them. Now it's your turn. Right from the start as you follow each step you will experience positive outcomes and plenty of improvements waiting for you, in your life, your work, your relationships and your joy of living.

Step 1 - Introduction

Aim: To gain a broad overall view of something that is going to take you a while to understand fully. As long as you get the general picture that's fine for now.

Q. What is an Unbalanced or Negative Core Belief like?

There are eleven or more groups with dozens of different '*because beliefs*' in each group.

Q. What do I need to know for a start?

None of those old beliefs are accurate. Most are not true, but telling you this, at this stage won't help much.

Core Beliefs are Unconscious

A core belief is more an energy state than a thought. It's stored in your body as well as your mind and no matter how hard people try they just don't seem to be able to work out what their core belief might,just by thinking it through rationally or analytically.

Starting with the "front end"

Beliefs such as *"I'm not good enough"* or or *"I am always wrong"* or *"I can't"* are good starting points that help lead you to your old core belief.

If that's what you identify for a start as an unbalanced core belief it's a good beginning. But, you still have a way to go, because every old core belief, and there are hundreds of them, all start out that way.

This book guides you from the start. It's an amazing do-it-yourself tool kit that you hold in your own hands and keep using for the rest of your life to enhance your self empowerment and love of being alive.

Here's a very brief outline of what you will be doing. It's explained in detail step by step, section by section throughout the book.

Understand what a core belief is like

Most troublesome core beliefs reflect a sense of *being or not being* than about not being able to *do things.* They will be about *"who I am"* or *"who I am not"* being rather than actions such as *"I always do it the wrong way"*

Here's an example: Imagine a core belief about *being powerless* You could start with "I can't" then try to identify the *core belief* as a ".... who I am" or ".... a "who I am not" belief for example *"I am powerless"* rather than *"I can't"*.

There are no common or one-size-fits-all old unbalanced core beliefs even though they begin with similar words like *"I am not good enough because* or *"I can't because I....."*

It is the words that follow your "*because I ...*" that tell you what your Core Belief is really about, your *core issue.* It's better if your actual belief doesn't end up including the word "because" but it helps to add it at this stage while you are searching for yours.

Fine tuning to get to the core

If at first there seem to be several closely connected beliefs some fine tuning may be needed. Example:

You might start with four beliefs *"I don't measure up" "I have no value" "I am nothing"* and *"I'm worthless."*

As you continue your core belief detective work the eight clues help bring a single *core issue* to the surface. All four are related to issues about being counted or measured or valued, particularly by people around you.

After a bit more detective work, your central belief turns out to be *"I don't count"* which is why it's described as the core.

That's when you notice that you had problems with arithmetic at school and even now you have trouble keeping track of your bank accounts. Those problems were all connected unconsciously to your central Core Belief and your core issue which is probably "counting".

After you balance a Core Belief like *"I don't count"* these problems settle down or even go away.

One thing that will not help

No matter how hard people try whether by reasoning, analysing, or just thinking and thinking and more thinking, they just don't seem to be able to work out what their old core belief is or what to do about it.

If that had been the answer you and I would have sorted it all out a long time ago.

Neither you nor a counsellor or a therapist can sort out a core belief using rational thinking or analysis alone. It's unconscious so you can't get far using conscious logic or reasoning.

I wasted more than fifty-five years and thousands in therapy in the grip of a core belief that I *had no value*. My rational mind (and mine is very good at analysing) could never see the problem, help me deal with it or make me feel valuable.

The thirty plus years since I named that (false) old belief and then balanced it have been the happiest and healthiest of my life.

Yes these days I really do feel and believe I am valuable.

Neither you nor a therapist or counsellor can remove an old core belief (but they can balance it with a positive one)

A Core Belief is Unconscious

It's an energy state in your body as well as in your mind. No matter how hard people try by thinking consciously about it, reasoning, analysing, they just don't seem to be able to work out what their old core belief is. People have very little long term success trying to discover a core belief using CBT processes.

Neither you nor the most skilled therapist can remove an old core belief

Not just your brain but in fact all your body cells hold your old belief. That old belief is hard wired, safely stored in places your logical mind can't get to. It has powerful restoration systems to put it back again and again no matter how often you might imagine you had managed to 'get rid of' it.

And that's good, because your old belief is still needed in the future. It will continue to play an essential part in your life and the more you accept this the more it can help you to live a balanced life. You keep it but by balancing it with an energetic opposite belief (also in your whole body) you gain the best of both sides.

Balance works better

Bringing balance back into your life is far more effective than trying to get rid of the old one, which isn't possible anyway and even if you could it certainly wouldn't help you because it would leave you out of balance feeling more positive than is natural.

Honouring and Appreciating

Honouring the old belief is an essential part of Core Belief work. The more you honour and express appreciation about what the old belief was doing originally to help in childhood and its five gifts the more you learn the truth about it. That makes it easier to balance it with its opposite more positive twin belief.

Even skilled therapists have very little success trying to deal with core beliefs using processes such as CBT. It just doesn't get to the place where your core belief lives inside you which is closer to your heart than your brain.

In this book I also explain why neither you nor a professional should ever try to remove a core belief completely. There are very good reasons why you don't want to totally "get rid of" yours. You need to keep parts of it, to maintain balance. There are other reasons as well.

Since it's still going to be around it's better to give it some new and more useful jobs that will keep it so busy it won't have time (or feel the need) to do the old negative stuff.

Why doesn't this look like a textbook?

Because it isn't meant to be one

Please don't see this book as the kind where you start at the beginning and plough through page by page until you get to the end. It's just not intended to be like that.

Read it instead like a magazine. Flip through the pages catching the key information in small boxes or in the illustrations.

Open it up at random, like a magazine. Whatever page you land on will have some information that will be relevant to things you are doing today.

I like to make my books more interesting to look at and easier to read. Where possible I introduce some light hearted comments and humour.

So go ahead and enjoy it the way I intended.

John Bligh Nutting

PS. I also invite you to take a pen and highlighter and colour, highlight and draw your way all the way through. Write your own comments on the page margins. Think of it as a workbook rather than a textbook.

You can always print another copy afterwards so you have an unmarked version.

Key terms used in this book

Balance, gift of balance
Old unbalanced beliefs, negative beliefs
Automatic over-reaction patterns
Triggers and trigger words
Outside of Me Intentions
Supporting beliefs
Expectations Forecasts Predictions Prophecies
Compensating skills
Core issues, issue words
Resonance
Authentic
Great law of energetic balance
Polar opposite energy, opposite energy states
Adverse Childhood Experiences ACEs
PYRO STAR and WING
Voice Dialogue
Key life skills
Vulnerability
Negative inventory, You are ..... messages

Signs I am driving under the influence of one or more of my Unbalanced Core Beliefs

1. So often things that I do or that people do with me seem to go wrong. What I expected did not happen. What I <u>didn't expect</u> was what happened (and it was not good).

2. Certain words, actions or events cause strong over-reactions - They're my 'trigger words or events'.

3. Triggered events like these happen to me regularly and they set me up so I over-reacti

4. Those over reactions patterns are repeated and have become all too familiar. These are described as 'F' reactions*. Fight, Fold, Flee, Fling, Flog, Floods of tears and many more. See note in the box below.

5. I wish I could change those repeated patterns but *I* don't seem able to. *"Why do people keep doing this to me?"* ; *"Why do I keep doing this?"*

6. Repeated conflict with family members, partners or a close friend.

7. All this supports a feeling inside me that whatever I need to fix my problems is *"outside of me"* - I can only change all this if someone or something else will change too.

8. I have little or no success, in spite of my most persistent efforts to get other people to change the negative things they do or say to me. That troubles me even more .

9. So, naturally, I find myself making forecasts, predictions, based on what happens so often, about how people are going to treat me and what I expect they will say or do to me,

10. I feel uncomfortable accepting compliments. Praise, appreciation or compliments (about me) leave me feeling a bit uneasy.

11. When I do achieve success it's only temporary. Somehow it doesn't remain for long.

12. I feel I have less and less of the resources (time, energy, money, health, skills etc.) I need right now to deal with immediate situations.

13. All this hurts deep inside me, like an un-healed emotional wound. This is my core pain. I try hard to hide or reduce the pain but any success is short lived.

14. The last thing I feel like doing is laughing about all this!

15. The "Over 35 sign" I am over 35 and these days things are not going as well as they used to - it's starting to look like I am headed for a mid-life crisis.

** Most F style over-reaction patterns have one common intention, to control other people, in the sense that we want to "make them" stop whatever they're doing that is triggering us. Yet we still feel surprised when <u>they</u> feel controlled by us or fight our attempts to control them.*

Starting your Detective work - **Triggered reactions**

<u>Aim:</u> Identifying some of your repeated self-defeating trigger patterns, over-reactions and other clues will help you start to create a picture of your own unbalanced belief. It helps to compare different types of F reactions and see why some kinds of reactions are grouped together.

Part Two - Even though it's hidden you can soon discover your own Core belief

Understand what it really is - Your first step was to understand some of the basic points, what a core belief is, and something about how it works. That's why we started with the previous pages. Later in this book it's all explained again in more detail but here's all you need to make a start discovering yours.

Look for signs, clues and pointers

Discovering your old unbalanced core belief does take a bit of work, and it's best of you do this step by step. It's not something you can work out just by thinking it through because core beliefs are hidden somewhere deeper in your unconscious mind. Rational analytical thinking cannot work there in the way it does when you are solving normal everyday problems.

Instead start collecting clues or pointers that indicate what kind of unbalanced old core belief might be at work in your system.

I describe you as working like a "Core Belief Detective."

Working Like an Core Detective

To discover your own individual unbalanced core belief you need to work like an Inner Detective. It's the only way I know that works as you investigate a number of different clues or pointers and put the results together to 'solve the case' and detect your own belief.

Different signs or clues that point you towards your own old unbalanced core belief:

There are some very significant clues that point you to the place where you will discover your own individual core belief:

- *Your Triggered or 'F' over-reactions and the trigger events that cause these strong reactions*
- *Your Beliefs about where you think power and control over your life are located (Do you still believe most real power is outside of you ? That's not true but as long as you still think that way your old belief is going to keep winning)*

Your Core beliefs are about:

- **who you are being or not being;**
- **what you are or what you are not;**
- **what you have or don't have;**

- *Your Predictions, Forecasts and Prophecies about what you expect to happen to you and what you expect people are going to do to you.*
- *Your very best career or work skills. The ones use that help you stand out in your work or career. They help you give special gifts to other people. Theyare called your Compensating skills and gifts*
- *Your Childhood and Family history*
- *Your discomfort with success and compliments*
- *Your Five Core Gifts*
- *Your Core Issue*

These pointers are each explained in more detail in this book as you look at each clue and see how it applies to you and your life. Book CBal-2 goes into more detail if you feel like making your discoveries at a more relaxed pace.

Your own core belief is specific and Individual

No two core beliefs are the same. Yours may have some similarities with mine but each one will be unique. It will not be the same as anyone else's.

I'll explain more about how an Inner detective works in the coming pages.

Do some Triggered or 'F' reactions Have a positive side?

Any sudden F reaction can cause problems but not all reactions are negative. F reactions are warning signs that tell you that you have once again been connected to your negative core belief.

Core Belief Balancing - Your Step by Step program

This is an outline of the work you'll be doing here, *but <u>only</u> if you choose to*, because self-empowerment is always do-it-yourself work. The steps are explained here, and there are do-it-youirself Activity sheets to guide you with each step.

A. Starting point

Explaining what a Core belief is and where it comes from. Problems when one is unbalanced. Ten Common patterns. Where yours came from (next page).

B. Discover yours. Why you need work like a Core Detective because you'll never get it by using reason or analytical logic. Are you driving under the influence of an old unbalanced core belief? Signs and a survey.

There are Eight clues that help you identify yours and 25 numbered Activity sheets to help you with each step.

Your first clue - your triggered over-reactions. Five Activity sheets to help you identify the triggers that hot wire you to your own core belief. Activity sheets CB-1 to CB-5.

Your second clue - The truth and the lies about Who you are and How Much you matter in the world. You are not 'your behaviour.' Blocking a negative inventory. Activity sheets CB-6 to CB-8

Your third clue - Your forecasts, expectations, prophecies and predictions can be influenced far too much by your old core belief.

However that makes them a very useful clue. Activity sheets CB-9 and CB-10.

Your fourth clue - How your skills and abilities create wonderful gifts (for other people) to help hide your core belief from them.

The specific kind of gifts *you choose* to give other people are usually the *opposite* of your core belief so they can be very useful clues. Activity sheets CB-11 and CB-12.

Your fifth clue- Your childhood and your family history. ACEs. Adverse Childhood Experiences. We all had some at least. They help set up core beliefs. CB-13.

Your sixth clue - If you are a bit uncomfortable with praise, compliments, success that's your core belief at work. CB-14.

Your seventh clue - Actually it's a positive inventory. There are five real gifts that your old core belief set up for you. Why you need to appreciate all five, especially the fifth gift.
Activity sheets CB-16 a CB-16 b and CB-16 c.

Your eighth clue - your core issue. Single Trigger words and issue words. CB-18 (there is no CB-17).

Getting ready to name your own core belief. Activity sheets CB-19 CB-20.

Finally - It's good to give your own core belief a name. Activity sheet CB-21 (two pages).

C. Next Getting ready for Balancing Identifying and embracing your Positive or opposite belief. Activity sheets CB-22 to CB-25.

D. After balancing. How do you know when it's working and how well it's working?

E. Additional reading

Your six Self aware grown up Life skills

Why it's important to balance your opposite energies.

Emotional Gym is the easiest way and fun.

Six areas of vulnerability

ACEs Adverse childhood experiences.

F. Emotional Age Awareness EA - The coloured EA wheel is a very important tool.

G. Where to next?

Talking to the author on Skype or Zoom.

Additional books.

These are Positive Processes

Core Belief Balancing and Emotional gym are very positive processes. As you work on each step you will experience positive outcomes and plenty of improvements that are waiting for you in your life, your work, your relationships and your joy of living.

They are each do-it-yourself processes

This book will guide you but in the end it is about a tool kit that you get to hold in your own hands and can use for the rest of your life to enhance your self empowerment and love of being alive.

Are you are reading this book on Kindle?

Here's a very special free gift, just for you

I have been publishing and distributing editions of this book for nearly 20 years. I'm excited now about distributing it through Amazon.

However there may be a minor problem for some of my new readers.

It's always been a workbook, which is why you'll find it includes more than 20 do-it-yourself Activity sheets. The traditional way to discover one's core belief was to write the survey scores and key answers to each activity sheet question straight into the spaces provided on that page. An equally good alternative was to make a copy, then write the scores and key answers on that copy.

Some people prefered to write theirs on blank paper, numbering the sheets to match the numbers of the original Activity sheets. Those ways each worked as long as they provided a permanent record of the scores and key answers.

Why you need to record your scores and answers to key questions somehow, somewhere.

That's because as you progress you need to refer back to the key answers you recorded in earlier sheets. Those records are also essential when it comes to the later stages of balancing your old belief with your new positive one. You can't do your balancing without them.

Thinking first, then making a permanent record is the only way which seems to work, that's if you want to discover your own unique but hidden core belief.

Many people have tried just reading and thinking about the questions but out of the hundreds I have worked with, not one has been successful naming their hidden belief let alone balancing it. That was until they recorded their survey scores and key answers somehow, somewhere, so they could refer back to them.

A free offer if you need it

If you can't print out the Activity sheets or if you would like a separate set to keep, apart from the ones in your book, please let me know. I have a special file with just the Activity sheets and it's yours. I am happy to e-mail as a pdf it *at no cost if* you contact me:

bligh4@growingaware.com

...... giving me the details of the date you purchased your Core Belief book from Amazon and please tell me whether it was a Kindle copy or an actual book. More free books. See page 116

Where do old Unbalanced Core Beliefs come from?

It all started a long time ago

Throughout the many different histories of civilisation human beings have always sought to create beliefs that helped them explain things for which there was no logical explanation.

Core beliefs are just one more example. Core beliefs are created very early in childhood as a young child's way of "making sense" of whatever they are experiencing even when it should not be happening to them.

An explanation for the unexplainable

Unbalanced Core Beliefs develop as a small child tries to work out a "because" to help them cope with something they don't understand or are troubled by in their daily life.

It might be neglect, injustice, dishonest parenting, parents with addictions, trauma, abuse or just feelings of vulnerability, fear or shame.

If the experiences were adverse the core belief you created as a child actually helped you fit in with your adverse environment.

Whatever a child is experiencing regularly the child feels the need for:

1. A "because" that would help them make sense of and accept what is happening to them *(even though it should not be happening).*

or

2. A "because" that will help them "fit in" better in their family or at school even though fitting in was not at all pleasant for them.

or both.

The primary reason for that belief coming into the child's system was to help the child cope, by providing an *explanation for the unexplainable.*

It needed to be about "me" the child

To make sense, the belief needed to include something about ***the child being responsible*** for their repeated adverse experiences. It could not be about what other "big" people were doing or not doing to the child.

The trouble is that the only "because" that seems to work (at that time) is backed up by the understandable belief held by most small children about the adults and elder siblings in the family.

"*.. it cannot be their fault. So it must be my fault."*

This in turn leads (in a small child's way) to the creation of the because behind a core belief:

"I am not good enough because I .....

"I can't because I don't know how .....

"I am not good enough because I am doing something the wrong way .... "

"I am a failure because ...."

"I am unlovable or shameful because ...."

"I must not allow myself to be seen because ...."

"I must not be heard because ...."

"I don't deserve to be happy because ...."

If believing any one of these 'because' thoughts increases the child's sense of *"fitting in"* and *"making sense"* of daily life as they know it, then (untrue though it is) this "because belief" will appear to be working for them, so every day the belief gets reinforced bur more as a feeling than actual words.

The more it seems to 'make sense' or help the child 'fit in' better, the more it seems in a small child's mind as though it *must be "true"* until it becomes firmly embedded.

At the time it was a necessity.

These are not Core Beliefs

If you can analyse, think logically through a belief, reverse it , get rid of, erase or remove that belief this confirms that it was <u>*not a core belief.*</u>

A belief that is about anyone or anything outside of you or what they will or won't do to you is <u>***not a core belief***</u>***.***

If there is even a suggestion that you might be better off obeying an old 'how to live rule' <u>*it is not a core belief.*</u> *Core beliefs do not offer choices or options.*

A belief that describes you as not doing or doing a specific action <u>***is not a core belief.***</u>

While it may seem strange to refer to this creation of the child's unbalanced core belief as a "gift" for the child at that time it was a necessity.

We describe this as a 'because' the child needed when they shouldn't have needed a 'because'.

In a functional family environment a child would not have needed to take on such negative beliefs about themselves.

Many core beliefs are pre-verbal

A core belief will often have been created in the pre-verbal child, or at best in a child with a very limited vocabilary. So, it will be embedded in the parts of the brain and the body that store emotions rather than words.

The words that describe the old belief may still not be clear but the energy will be very powerful. So that's another reason why you need to stop looking for words or using logical left brain analysis in an attempt to "think" the right words to describe what your your core belief might be. It can't work.

Instead you need to work like a detective, looking for physical clues starting with your triggered events.

Core Belief work is NOT Therapy. It cannot 'heal' nor 'cure' nor 'fix'

Self awareness and self empowerment are powerful processes. But they are NOT therapy and must never be presented as if they were therapeutic in nature or intention. The activities in this book are in no way suggested as a cure nor treatment for any diagnosable condition, whether physical or psychological in nature.

They may however compliment other treatments by helping you develop a more positive outlook about yourself, your body, your self-esteem and your authentic vulnerability.

If a diagnosable condition is partly related to non-physical or ACE issues the chances of improvement are then likely to increase.

The difference between an Ordinary Negative belief and a Core belief

We all have beliefs, lots and lots of them. That's pretty natural. Many of them are about what you should or should not do around other people, not so much about who you are or what you feel about yourself. For example:

1. Positive Beliefs about how to live life

Some positive beliefs are handed to us by our parents, others are given to us by teachers, spiritual leaders, grandparents, friends and of course the mass media as we listen, read, watch and learn.

Many positive beliefs started out as opinions but because they are positive and if they are explained carefully and make sense we come to accept them and believe them. They help us develop our personality, our values and positive ways of dealing with life.

Faced with reliable evidence over a period of time these positive beliefs can grow, change or alter.

Something similar can happen with spiritual beliefs which are even stronger but even these can change as we grow up. None of these are core beliefs.

2. Negative Beliefs or rules - about how we should <u>not live life</u> are not core beliefs.

Other opinions can be negative, but if they are presented strongly enough by people whose opinions we trust they too become beliefs. Look at these examples of beliefs which are both false and negative, rules about how we should not live life.

Starting in childhood we can accept them and follow them as unquestioned rules for life.

Caring for myself is selfish.

I must not I put myself ahead of others.

All anger is bad

Don't trust people who are different.

People who like themselves are not nice.

It's rude to say 'No' to friends.

> *If you can reverse, get rid of, erase or remove a negative belief this confirms that it is **not a core belief**.*
>
> ***A belief that is about anyone or anything outside of me is not a core belief.***

However as we grow up, we can take a long hard look at those negative beliefs and discover we are able to change them or even reject them.

These negative rules are usually not true. They only remain beliefs for as long as we don't question them. They are not the same as core beliefs.

Here are some signs that identify these as ordinary negative beliefs <u>but not core</u> beliefs.

* They are more likely to be about what you should or should not do around other people.
* You can think about them. The more you think about them the easier it is to name them as beliefs and then question them.
* You can look at and listen to reliable evidence that questions the truth of that belief.
* Then, if you notice that a belief is too negative, more harmful than helpful, you can use sensible, rational analytical thinking to alter that belief.
* Attached to this kind of negative belief is a hidden message about what might happen to us if we did not follow it. A core belief doesn't offer you that option.

Ordinary negative beliefs like the examples above can be changed, reversed or even rejected completely as long as we have enough solid evidence to support the change. We took them on as a result of what we believed about them at some earlier time. If we are presented with sufficiently strong , reliable, factual evidence that they are no longer true, we can change those ordinary negative beliefs.

3. A belief that is about anyone or anything outside of me is not a core belief.

When people start to identify their negative beliefs it's understandable that the more obvious thoughts will come to the surface.

Examples: *Nobody loves me; People don't trust me, I must not trust anyone. I'm not understood, People can see I am defective, Nobody can heal my pain, No one can see me. I will be rejected.*

Beliefs like these point to a deeper core belief which will be about me, but my core belief will not be this kind of forecast or prediction about what other people will or will not do to me.

4. That's where core beliefs are so different.

Core beliefs are about what you are or what you are not, about what you have or don't have, about who you are being or not being.

I am unlovable;
I am guilty;
I am always wrong;
I am defective;
I will fail;
I have no value;
I am not visible;
I am powerless;
I have no hope;
I am a reject;
I'm not authentic

* They are never about other people, never about things or events. They are only about me, because they are inside me.
* A belief that describes you doing or not doing, a specific action is not a core belief.
* They are much deeper, much harder to think about and at the same time far more persistent and more powerful.
* Evidence that should cause us to question a negative core belief is usually rejected.
* Evidence no matter how shallow that appears to support the negative core belief is usually accepted without question or even embraced.
* Sensible, rational analytical thinking is seldom able to make any real change to a core belief. If it does appear to have made a change this is usually short lived and soon reversed.
* Core beliefs do not change or go away. But they do respond to dynamic energetic balancing. Rather than changing them, balancing alters their role in the system so they play more useful part as a counter balance for the positive belief.
* It is a mistake even to try to get rid of a negative core belief. You need to keep it in order to balance it with your positive belief.

Core beliefs are about:

- **who you are being or not being;**
- **what you are or what you are not,**
- **what you have or don't have;**

Balancing anything inside us by embracing their positive and negative sides is a normal natural process. It is how we are supposed to manage our life.

So if someone says they are able to reverse, get rid of or reject a negative belief, and particularly if they say they were able to do this using sensible rational analytical thinking, that simply confirms that *it could not have been a core belief.*

5. A belief that *"I'm not good enough."* or *"I will be rejected."* is only a starting point that helps to lead you to your negative core belief.

If that's what you identify for a start as a negative core belief that's a very good beginning. But, you still have a way to go, because every negative core belief and there are hundreds of them, often sound like that at the beginning of a search.

If you look at the many examples of core beliefs in this book you can see why it's so important to keep digging until you can identify the actual core issue, the part that gets triggered and which is embedded deeper inside you.

Identifying your core issue and core belief starts when you add the word "because" to the statement "I'm not good enough."

Once you can name your belief including the words that follow after your "because" that's when it starts to lose its power over you. When you balance it with a positive belief you reach a point where one day you can actually laugh about it.

You will then no longer feel the old "I'm not good enough" feeling, but the total rewards will go far deeper.

Your life will be far more positive and more powerful.

You will feel a lot happier inside yourself and a lot more than just "good enough."

Your unbalanced core beliefs tell you that who you are and how much you matter is determined by other people, not by you. This is untrue.

To discover your own individual old core belief you need to .....

Work Like an Inner Detective

To discover your own individual old core belief you work like an Inner Detective. It's the only way I know that works. You can detect your own core belief by following eight different clues or pointers and then put the results together to 'solve the case.'

To make this easier I have spent the last 18 years developing a set of Activity Sheets to help you pinpoint the ways each of those clues might apply in your own life.

Each Activity sheet asks you a series of questions and each one of your answers takes you one step closer to discovering just what your own individual old core belief is about.

Feedback from all over the world assures me that this kind of inner detective work, using the activity sheets works surprisingly well.

Thousands of people here in Australia and in many other countries have discovered their individual old core beliefs using the sheets.

On the following pages you'll find a set of guidelines so you can follow the same steps and start the positive process of discovering your own belief, using the activity sheets in this book.

Work at your own pace

The activity sheets are designed so you can work on your own at your own pace. Don't rush things but at the same time don't spend a lot of time on any one question.

Beliefs such as *"I'm not good enough"* or or *"I am always wrong"* or *"I can't"* are good starting points that help lead you to your old core belief.

If that's what you identify for a start as an unbalanced core belief that's a very good beginning. But, you still have a way to go, because every old core belief and there are hundreds of them, *all start that way*

Inner Detective Guide

First Clue - triggered reactions

Triggered over-reactions are the most obvious clues that an unbalanced core belief is 'at work' inside you or in another person.

Advanced Detective work

Each of these will give you one particular sign, clue or pointer to help you identify your own old Core Belief.

Second clue- You're stuck with a false belief that most power is held by other people and that power is outside of you.

Third Clue - Prophecies, Predictions Expectations and Forecasts

Fourth Clue - Compensating skills and gifts.

Fifth Clue - Family History

Sixth Clue - you're uncomfortable receiving (some kinds of) compliments and/or can't handle sucess. If it happens occasionally it doesn't stay with you permanently.

Seventh Clue - The Five Core Gifts

Eighth Clue - Your Core Issue and your Trigger words

Just respond with whatever you think or feel at that moment or by saying how much you feel each statement applies to you at present.

As you work on some sheets you may experience various levels of discomfort. Many people feel sad, tired or angry at some point.

If those feelings becomes too strong, it could be a sign that you need to do more reading, and come back to those activity sheets later.

Take a break and have a look at the case study at the end of this book. There are four more case studies in Book CBal-2.

Case Studies are More Fun

Working through a case study will give you a good idea of how a core detective goes about the task of discovering a hidden core belief. The case history in this book is loaded with obvious clues about the character's core belief, so it is not too hard to work out what his or hers might be.

When you get back to you activity sheets, you should find it easier get to work detecting your own eight clues and naming your own core belief.

Then you can move on to the belief balancing process.

Detecting Your own Unbalanced Negative Core Belief

Step by Step

1. What signs or clues give you the feeling that you that you might have an unbalanced core belief inside?

Read the list "*Signs that tell you that you are under the influence of one or more negative core beliefs then* complete Activity sheet 'CB-1' the starting point of your Unbalanced Core Belief Detector kit.

2. Identify your most commonly repeated over-reactions. Your first clue.

Start by describing some of the problems an unknown yet powerful unbalanced old core belief seem to be causing in your life, damaging your careers, wrecking relationships and reducing self-esteem at the same time as helping reduce your personal wealth and affecting your health.

Make a list of what actually happens when you over-react, particularly the kinds of reactions you repeat most often and which seem to do the most damage in terms of your friendships and relationships. The Activity sheets in this Book will help here.

3. Give your highest scoring reactions easy to remember names

If the ready-made names from the list in this book seem to fit for you, use them. If not make up your own label. Your labels do not need to begin with the letter F. If you've already completed activity sheets CB-1 to CB-5 you know which ones are your highest scoring reactions.

4. Identify the trigger event, whatever is happening just before your over-reaction starts.

Look for a common theme or a similarity in each situation, something which you could describe as one of your triggers. The Activity sheets CB-4(a) and CB-4(b) will help here.

5. **What issues seem to be outside you are really inside you? Your second clue**

Can you start to see is how often you have tried to hide all this from other people and yet at the same time wanted them to change to help you feel better about yourself.

Trying to get others to change so you will feel better about your belief is a waste of your time and theirs too. Use your Activity sheets in this book to highlight what you might have been trying to hide from other people and what you might have been trying to get from other people in order to have them to help you deal with *your belief.*

Eight Clues that help Identify a Core Belief

1. *Your triggered F Reactions*
2. *Your old "Power is Outside of me" rule*
3. *Your Prophecies Predictions Forecasts*
4. *Gifts you give away to Compensate*
5. *Your Family History*
6. *Discomfort accepting compliments/success*
7. *Your Five Core Gifts*
8. *Your Core issue*

6. **What are your predicting, forecasting or similar supporting beliefs? Your third clue.**
What do you predict or expect that other people will do to you that will then trigger an over-reaction in you? Those predictions might send out advance non-verbal signals to other people about your negative core belief. Use Activity sheets **CB-9**

7. List your compensating skills. Your fourth clue
Often these are the mirror opposite of your negative core belief which is telling you about what you are or are not, or why you are not good enough.

Your compensating skills are the things you do to show other people that you really are good enough. (Activity sheets CB-11 and CB-12)

8. See if you can make a connection between what's happening to you, your triggers and your childhood history. Your fifth clue
There will always be a connection between what's happening to you in your life, your triggers and your childhood history. Your own core belief was created inside you because it was needed to help you "fit in with" or "make sense of" things that were happening to you in your childhood.

In your particular case how would you have needed to adapt or change your beliefs about yourself to help you 'fit in' better with your family or 'make sense' of what was happening to you as a small child? (Activity sheet CB-13)

Can you link your childhood history with the first gift you received from your Unbalanced Core belief? (This is explained in more detail under the heading "Five Gifts" and (Activity sheets CB-15 and CB-16)

9. What kind of compliments or praise do you find difficult accepting? Sixth Clue

One of the ways to identify a core belief is just to ask yourself what kind of compliment (about you) usually makes you feel most uncomfortable

10. There are five gifts that your old Core belief gives you. Seventh clue.

Helping you fit in or make sense of life as a child is the first gift. Your compensating skills were the second gift. If you're not clear yet why these were gifts or about the other three gifts you may need to skip this step for the time being.

11. Suggest one or two possible *core issues* that you can relate to. Eighth Clue

Look for one or two words that summarise what's troubling you inside when you're triggered. What words or themes keep appearing in your activity sheets, your childhood history and in the theme or focus of your compensating skills, your predictions about what others will do to you and what you do to try to prevent them doing.

The list of core issues and trigger words and Activity sheets CB17 and CB-18 may be a help at this point.

12. When you're ready refer to the General Core Belief pattern list (below).

Identify just one or two of the eleven different broad kinds of negative core belief that you feel might be close to your own core belief.

Make a note of two or three of the headings which you feel cause the strongest reaction inside you.

13. Go to the long list of different beliefs.

Look at the various individual beliefs listed under the eleven headings in the table below but in more detail. **(pages 12 to 14)** Are there one or two beliefs on that list that cause an immediate reaction or seem to ring a bell for you and that reflect the words of your core issue?

14. Experiment writing out different unbalanced or negative beliefs.

Activity sheet CB-21 will help you here. Try using your core issue words in different ways as you write. Try writing *"I am not good enough because I ...."* or *"I am always wrong because I ...."* and *"I can't because I ....".*

Do any of these phrases seem to resonate inside you. These are signs that you are getting closer to your unbalanced or negative core belief.

15. Notice just how many ways the old belief seems to have controlled your daily life, choice of career and relationships.

The more you notice about its effect on your life the closer you're getting to naming it.

16. Try naming what you think might be your old unbalanced belief.

You will discover that just being able to name the old unbalanced belief reduces its power over you. Saying it this way *does not make it stronger*, as long as you identify it as 'my old unbalanced *(rather than 'negative')* core belief' and add the words ..... *"but it has now lost its power over me"*.

17. Get ready to identify your positive belief and then to balance it with your old negative one

Get ready, to discover how being able to balance your two beliefs is a wonderful gift, just waiting for you to claim it.

Get ready to feel the empowerment that comes with the realisation that everything you need to sort it is inside you or in your hands.

How you do this is explained in detail in Book CBal-3.

Meanwhile from this day on you'll begin to notice and understand more and more about your old negative core belief and how it has affected your life.

18. When you feel ready you'll find yourself starting to laugh about all this.

Unbalanced Negative core beliefs - general patterns

Unbalanced negative beliefs can be very different from person to person. Some are quite unique. Most core beliefs however are connected in a broad way with a sense of having no power, no self worth or not being good enough:

Old Core Belief Patterns	Core Issues
1. Not good enough (I am not safe)	Security Safety
2. Not good enough (I don't belong)	Belonging, Nurture Self care
3. Not good enough (I have no value, I am worthless)	Self worth
4. Not good enough (I am powerless, I have no value)	Strength, Success, Power Control
5. Not good enough (I am wrong, I am unsure)	Reality; Reason Sanity, Knowing
6. Not good enough (My life is out of balance)	Balance Moderation
7. Not good enough (I don't exist; I am nothing)	Identity; Self, Recognition
8. Not good enough (I am not real)	Self awareness, Sanity
9. Not good enough (I am unlovable; left out; unwanted)	Love, Loved and Loving
10. Not good enough (I am defective)	Health; Self healing, Strength
11. Not good enough (I am not whole I have lost my spirit)	Wholeness; Spirit

Activity Sheet CB-1

Keep this sheet private - Show it only to your therapist or counsellor or to close friends who will respect your confidentiality

Date _ _/ _ _/ _ _

Negative Core Belief Detector

Work fast. Do not spend a lot of time on any one reaction. **Only score the ones you do more often.** *If you feel your score on any line is between 1 to 4 then score a zero. But, if you feel your score is on the red 5 to 10 side just pick one number somewhere between 5 and 10 that you think or feel might indicate how each statement applies to you at present. Accurate scoring is not necessary. Wondering whether 6 or 7? - 8 or 9? Either one will give the same results.*

1. How often do things that you do ***for*** other people seem to go wrong.

Seldom or never 0_ 1_ 2_ 3_ 4 _5_ 6_7_ 8_ 9_10 Almost all the time

2. How often do things that you do ***with*** *other people* **s**eem to go wrong.

Seldom or never 0_ 1_ 2_ 3_ 4 _5_ 6_7_ 8_ 9_10 Almost all the time

3. Certain words, actions or events seem to 'trigger' you. A *trigger* is anything that fires you up or causes a sudden strong reaction, a word, an event, a phrase, an action, a specific comment, a specific experience, an action by another person. *It can be a particular sight or sound, a sudden flash of a past memory, a tone of voice. Or it can be something you really hoped for or expected that did not happen. When this happens to me.....*

I don't react much at all 0_ 1_ 2_ 3_ 4 _5_ 6_7_ 8_ 9_10 I get triggered too often

4. If you experience your own individual trigger events again and again you develop ***regular, repeated reaction patterns***. (Anger, sadness, surrender, running away, fighting, cannons, crucifixes, concrete) Your most commonly repeated reactions are described as your "F" patterns. Your "F" reaction patterns use up a lot of energy.

I don't have any strong "F" patterns 0_ 1_ 2_ 3_ 4 _5_ 6_7_ 8_ 9_10 I have strong "F" reactions

5. Repeated conflict with family members, partners or a close friend.

Seldom or never 0_ 1_ 2_ 3_ 4 _5_ 6_7_ 8_ 9_10 A familiar pattern in my life

6. You often feel blocked or stuck or just don't get round to doing things you really want to do. You want to change but often find you just don't get round to making that change.

I never get stuck or not able to change 0_ 1_ 2_ 3_ 4 _5_ 6_7_ 8_ 9_10 Can't change Stuck Can't move

7. All this adds to a feeling inside that whatever I need to fix my problems is *"outside of me"* or that I can improve my life with the right help from someone else.

All the answers are inside me 0_ 1_ 2_ 3_ 4 _5_ 6_7_ 8_ 9_10 It's they who make the problems, not me

8. You try to get other people to change the things they do or say that trigger you because they cause you so much trouble but with little success.

They usually change 0_ 1_ 2_ 3_ 4 _5_ 6_7_ 8_ 9_10 They never change

9. If these things keep happening most people start making forecasts or predictions about how they are going to be treated by others, what they expect others will say or do. Looking back on your past experiences or your own repeated patterns how often do you make forecasts or predictions such as "it's going to happen again" or "nothing ever works for me"?

I seldom or never predict problems 0_ 1_ 2_ 3_ 4 _5_ 6_7_ 8_ 9_10 I make lots of forecasts like that

10. I feel uncomfortable accepting compliments or praise for something I have done well

Seldom or never 0_ 1_ 2_ 3_ 4 _5_ 6_7_ 8_ 9_10 Most of the time

11. Do you have a feeling you have less and less of the resources (time, energy, money, health, skills etc.) that you need to deal with life. That leaves you feeling more vulnerable, defeated or overwhelmed or just lost. How often do you feel this way?

Seldom or never 0_ 1_ 2_ 3_ 4 _5_ 6_7_ 8_ 9_10 Most of the time

12. All this hurts you deep inside like an unhealed wound

Does not apply to me 0_ 1_ 2_ 3_ 4 _5_ 6_7_ 8_ 9_10 I feel that pain so often

13. This is more likely to apply if you are over 35 years of age. Looking back you can see that during your twenties and early thirties your life, your relationships and your career were quite successful, but now things are not going as well. It is harder to start a new project even though you really want to. Or you get started but then can't finish it for ages and ages.

Does not apply to me 0_ 1_ 2_ 3_ 4 _5_ 6_7_ 8_ 9_10 True for me

Total your scores for all 13 questions above _ _ _ _ _ Transfer this total to **page 39** to get your detector rating

Examples of Common Unbalanced Core Beliefs

Most negative core beliefs are connected in a broad way with a feeling of lost self worth or of not being "good enough because ....." but it is the words that follow this phrase which are the most powerful.

They describe your core issue and those two or three words can set up a negative pattern that you will bond to and repeat throughout your life, until you can balance it with a positive pattern.

A supporting belief is a similar prediction, forecast or prophecy about what other people will or won't do to you. It is not a core belief but it is closely linked.

Note: The same belief can often appear under two or more headings

1. Not good enough (I am not safe) because

I'm unprotected
I am afraid
I am vulnerable
I am helpless
I hurt other people

Predicting, Forecasting or Supporting beliefs and predictions
Nobody will protect me
Linked Issues
Safety; Security; Peace; harmony; vulnerability; protection

2. Not good enough (I don't belong) because

I am unwelcome
I don't fit in anywhere
I am lost
I am all alone
I can't help myself
I am unwanted
I should not be here at all
I am not allowed / to speak / to be me / to be free
I don't deserve

Predicting, Forecasting or Supporting beliefs
Nobody wants to know about me
Linked Issues
Belonging; Connection; self-nurturing

3. Not good enough (I have no value, I am worthless) I am disposable because

I am unworthy
I am not worth anything
I am not worth listening to
I am not interesting enough
I am no good
I never come first
I always come second
I'm nothing
I'm not valuable
I am uninteresting
I am unimportant
I'm not anybody

Predicting, Forecasting or Supporting beliefs
Nobody values me
Nobody cares about me
People who say nice things to me don't mean them

Linked Issues
Self worth; Loyalty, Difficulty giving or receiving gifts, congratulations, love or appreciation;

4. Not good enough (I am powerless) because

I am incompetent
I am not any good
I am unsuccessful
I am inferior
I can't control anything
I am disposable
I am unworthy
I can't achieve
I can't change
It's no use (me) trying
There is no way out for me
I can't help myself

Do one or two beliefs here seem to "jump out at you"?

If one or two of the beliefs on this list seem to "jump out at you" today, mark them so you can look back at them later. They may not be your specific core beliefs but they could be important clues.

Beliefs such as *"I'm not good enough"* or or *"I am always wrong"* or *"I can't"* are good starting points that help lead you to your old unbalanced core belief.

If they are what you identify for a start as your unbalanced core beliefs that's a good beginning. But, you still have a way to go, because every negative core belief and there are hundreds of them, all start that way.

False belief - I would feel much better inside, if only I could make the world and the people "outside me" treat me better

Predicting, Forecasting or Supporting beliefs

Other people manipulate me and control my life

I am trapped and cannot escape. I will never be permitted to be the real me. I will fail

I will never become the real "me"

If I dare to ___ *(any action)* ____

I wiil be punished.

Linked issues

Achievement; Boundaries; Standards; Structure; Success; Goals, Results; Being organised, Self empowerment; ability to make changes; bonding patterns; self-protection; avoiding manipulation;

Unbalanced Negative core beliefs - general patterns

Unbalanced negative beliefs can be very different from person to person. Some are quite unique. Most core beliefs however are connected in a broad way with a sense of having no power, no self worth or not being good enough:

Old Core Belief Patterns	Core Issues
1. Not good enough (I am not safe)	Security Safety
2. Not good enough (I don't belong)	Belonging, Nurture Self care
3. Not good enough (I have no value, I am worthless)	Self worth
4. Not good enough (I am powerless, I have no value)	Strength, Success, Power Control
5. Not good enough (I am wrong, I am unsure)	Reality; Reason Sanity, Knowing
6. Not good enough (My life is out of balance)	Balance Moderation
7. Not good enough (I don't exist; I am nothing)	Identity; Self, Recognition
8. Not good enough (I am not real)	Self awareness, Sanity
9. Not good enough (I am unlovable; left out; unwanted)	Love, Loved and Loving
10. Not good enough (I am defective)	Health; Self healing, Strength
11. Not good enough (I am not whole I have lost my spirit)	Wholeness; Spirit

5. Not good enough (I am wrong, I am unsure) because

I don't know
I always get it wrong
I am always wrong
I am confused
I can't understand
I'm not understood
I can't be sure
I am in the wrong place
I am a mistake
I am unaware
I am uncertain
I can't make myself clear
I am mistaken
I am not trustworthy

Predicting, Forecasting or Supporting beliefs

It isn't fair
I won't get justice
I can't trust people
People don't trust me
I am not understood

Linked Issues

Truth; Right-wrong; Justice; Fairness; Openness and honesty; Trust and Trustworthiness; Integrity; Understanding

6. Not good enough (My life is out of balance)

I am unbalanced
I am out of control
I can't be moderate
I always get it wrong
Nothing works for me
I stuff up everything I do
I am a klutz
I can't fix it
Everything I do goes wrong
I attract trouble
My life is just not working
I have ruined my whole life
I can't get it right
I am in the wrong place
I can't make it work (klutz)
I can't fix it
I will never be able to fix it up

Predicting, Forecasting or Supporting beliefs

Other people have to fix my life for me

Wherever I am I don't like it. I need to move

Linked Issues

Success; Fixing problems; Solutions; Achievement;

7. Not good enough (I don't exist, I am nothing)

I am nothing
I am worthless
I am invisible
I don't exist
I'm nothing
I'm not anybody
I am insignificant
I am not enough
I am not recognised

Predicting, Forecasting or Supporting beliefs

People cannot see me

Linked Issues

Recognition; Being who I really am; My history; My knowledge; My experience; Self-awareness; My doings are not my beings (Who I am is not what I do)

8. Not good enough (I am not real)

I am a fake
I don't know what is real
I am unsuitable
I am not true
I don't know who I really am
I am not visible
I am not seen

Predicting, Forecasting or Supporting beliefs

People will find out that I am a fake

Linked Issues

Freedom; Autonomy; Individuality; intimacy; self-protection; Balancing my personal and impersonal energies

9. Not good enough (I am unlovable; unwanted I don't belong)

I am not lovable
I don't matter
I am not special
I don't belong

I am unacceptable
I don't matter
I am alone
I am unwelcome
I don't fit in anywhere
I am unsuitable
I am uninteresting
I am unimportant

Predicting, Forecasting or Supporting beliefs
Nobody loves me
Nobody wants me
I am always left out
I am not wanted

Linked Issues

Caring; Sharing; Unconditional loving; Balancing my giving and receiving;

10. Not good enough (I am defective) because
I am no good
I am crazy
I am unfixable, unrepairable
I am damaged goods
I am bad
I am imperfect
I am inadequate
I am guilty
It's my fault
I am not whole
I am unattractive
I am stupid
I am awkward
I am slow
I can't be me
I am hopeless
I'm not true
I'm dirty
I am ugly
I am fat
I'm shameful
I am unclean
I am useless
I am a reject
I am crazy
I am unbalanced
I will fail
I am a failure
I am a fraud or a fake
I am flawed, a reject
I am stupid
I am useless
I am always sad
I am a reject
I am a loser
I will lose it all
It's all my fault
I am plain and dull
I don't deserve to be me
I don't deserve to be loved
I don't deserve anything
There's something very wrong with me
Everything I do goes wrong
I don't deserve to be loved
I don't deserve to be me
I don't deserve to live
I don't deserve to be cared for
I don't deserve to be me
I don't deserve to be loved
I don't deserve anything
There's something terribly wrong with me

Predicting, Forecasting or Supporting beliefs
I am hurting, in pain
People can see that I am defective
People can tell there is something wrong with me
They will discover I am a fraud or a fake.
Someone else needs to heal, fix or repair me
Unless you heal me I will never get better
Nobody can heal my pain
Don't trust anybody

Linked Issues
Self healing, defects; perfection, pain ;Integrity; Logic and Reason; Balancing giving and receiving; Emotional age; Growth; Avoiding "flips" between opposite positions; morality

11. Not good enough (I have lost my spirit) because
I am not whole
I have no integrity
I have no hope
I feel hopeless
I have lost my spirit
I am a bad person
I am sinful
I am evil
I can't grow

Predicting, Forecasting or Supporting beliefs
There is nothing to hope for
I must not get my hopes up
Nothing good ever happens to me

Linked Issues
Integrity; Balance Wholeness; Spirit; Self-actualisation; Spirit and spirituality; Personal Growth; morality; ethics; principles;

Eight Clues that help Identify a hidden Core Belief

1. *Your triggered F Reactions*
2. *Your old "Power is Outside of me" rule*
3. *Your Prophecies Predictions Forecasts*
4. *Gifts you give away to Compensate*
5. *Your Family History*
6. *Discomfort accepting compliments/success*
7. *Your Core Gifts*
8. *Your Core issue*

Your unbalanced core beliefs tell you that who you are and how much you matter is determined by other people, not by you. This is untrue.

If you complete the Core Belief Detector sheets and then the other Activity sheets numbered CB-1 to CB-18 in this book you'll almost certainly be able to identify your own unique Unbalanced old Core belief.
If you are still not sure then please e-mail me bligh4@growingaware.com and I'll help. Your first personal on line session is always free.

Additional problems

But Wait, There's More

.....and each one is somehow connected to your core belief

With core beliefs there are some additional problems that seem to come with the core belief. They aren't caused by the core belief but having a core belief does make them likely to create additional trouble.

If these extra problems are associated with old negative core beliefs it's because they were set up by the same childhood problems that led to the formation of the your core beliefs.

Your core belief is likely to make them worse. And they can hurt you a lot more because of your core belief.

The good news is that after you balance your core belief these additional problems seem to settle down as well.

They are all outcomes of what are today recognised as 'ACEs' that is Adverse Childhood Experiences. A few years ago there was very little to be found on the internet about ACEs. Now there are hundreds of pages. Google ACEs to see for yourself.

The more ACEs you experienced back then the more problems you have in adult life.

Health problems and body pain

Overweight
Poor diet
Anorexia
Headache or back ache

Emotional issues

Stress and Anxiety
Feeling unbalanced
High blood pressure
Rapid and wide mood swings
Negativity, depression, feeling too tired

Relationship issues

Repeated relationship breakdowns - divorce
Constant blaming and arguments
Infidelity - affairs (you or your partner)

Problems with Career or Profession

Business Failure or loss
Stalled career, no promotions no advancement

The good news is that after you balance your core beliefs many of these extra problems seem to settle down as well.

Major Life Choices later turn out to be big mistakes

Wrong marriage, wrong career, wrong life style
Poor decision Making Choosing the wrong solution
Muddled thought processes

Over Medicating

Substances - alcohol - nicotine - drugs
Process - gambling - debt - love addiction
Workaholic patterns

Financial problems

High Debt
Loss of income

How do I know about this?

Because out of this list, at different times in my life I experienced at least three quarters of those. I now recognise that as well as a negative core belief that I had no value I also had a high childhood ACE score and I in my case I can see the connection clearly.

That was until twenty two years ago, when I had a major heart attack followed by a quadruple by-pass heart operation.

Three months later while still recovering I found out about my negative core belief. I balanced it with a positive one. Things have gone so much better for me ever since.

Actually, the last twenty years have been the happiest and the healthiest of my life.

Usually there is a connection between a strong negative core belief and a history of too may Adverse Childhood Experiences or ACEs.

There will always be a connection between a strong negative core belief and childhood based PTSD.

Your First Clue Discover Your Most Powerful Triggered or 'F" Reaction patterns

A trigger can be an event, a phrase, an action, a specific comment, a specific experience, an action by another person. It can be a particular sight or sound. Another person's emotion (someone else's fear, pain or anger or just their tone of voice) is often a trigger.

Before you can start to balance your negative core beliefs you need to become familiar with the warning signs that tell you that you have been hot wired to your negative core belief and once that happens it can take control of almost everything you say and do!

Your own individual Triggered or 'F' reactions are the first and most easily noticeable signs that alert you to what is happening.

Learn to recognise these reactions and think of them like red warning lights that flash to help you become more aware of the way your negative core beliefs operate inside you. You can learn a great deal about your core beliefs just by observing these repetitive patterns, even before you know exactly what your core beliefs are.

The more experience you get doing this the more quickly you can stop them taking over automatically and creating problems for you.

Your triggered F reactions - **Activity sheet CB-2**

Aim: Making your own list of your triggered over-reaction patterns (your own "F" patterns).

As you identify some of your more common repeated self-defeating trigger patterns and over-reactions you start collecting clues about your own unbalanced belief.

Expect your scores to be different from anyone else's because your F reaction patterns are unique to you. That helps you pinpoint the kind of things that uniquely trigger you.

Your highest scoring groups point to the core belief groups or types of triggers that affect you the most both in intensity and the way they happen more often. Both are useful clues for you.

Each reaction is helping to remind you that something inside you is being kept busy protecting you from the same core pain that is connected to your same old negative core belief.

That was the unbalanced belief which helped in the past to set up your automatic everyday ways of dealing with life's problems.

Knowing and naming your own individual reaction patterns also helps you discover the unique core beliefs behind each of these patterns. (Activity sheets CB-2, CB-4 (a) and 4 (b) and CB-5)

The examples on the next twelve pages will help you to identify your reactions and responses which in turn will help you identify your negative core beliefs.

Traditionally the two best known F reactions are "fight" or "flight" but there are many more.

Starting your Detective work - **Triggered reactions**

Aim: Identifying some of your repeated self-defeating trigger patterns, over-reactions and other clues will help you create a picture of your own unbalanced belief. It helps to compare different types of F reactions and see why some kinds of reactions are grouped together.

Most F style over-reaction patterns have one common intention, to control other people, in the sense that we want to "make them" stop whatever they're doing that triggers us. Yet we still feel surprised when other people feel controlled or they fight our control. That's their reaction or, in most cases, their over-reaction in response to our over reaction

What is a "trigger" and what is "triggering"?

A trigger can be an event, a phrase, an action, a specific comment, a specific experience, an action by another person. It can be a particular sight or sound. Another person's emotion (someone else's fear, pain or anger or just their tone of voice) is often a trigger.

When it happens you are hot wired straight to your negative core belief and the childhood memories associated with it. It's automatic, you can't stop it and it's fast.

Triggers are often reminders

Some of your triggers have been with you all your life; many have been there since early childhood and they set off the same reaction each time you're reminded of the original situation.

A sudden flash of a past memory, hearing a familiar phrase, a long remembered piece of music, a particular aroma (a familiar perfume) or being touched somewhere on your body can trigger very strong reactions if these events connect you to a Core Belief and to your past.

Even just talking about a painful past event can trigger you.

Non-events can trigger you too

A trigger event can just as easily be anything you hoped for which did not happen. All it needs is a non event (Example: being ignored) which reminds you of your childhood wounding when you were constantly ignored or neglected, (your core pain) and you are triggered again.

It may be a word or a phrase you really want to hear, but remains unsaid. If there is an event or an action you really, really want so much and it doesn't occur that too can hot wire you to your negative core belief. These are all very common as triggers.

Examples of triggers

When you are identifying your trigger events it helps to think of specific examples like *'When I was blamed for losing the money'* rather than *'I'm always being blamed for losing things'*.

Many trigger events are about being criticised, blamed or controlled or some injustice:

When .... (name of person)..... criticised me;

When .... (name of person).... told me I was .....;

When........ (name of person)..... was so unfair about .....;

When I was forced to . (something I did not want to do)....;

When .... (name of person).... blamed me for ... (something I did not do)......;

When....... (name of person).....yelled at me and lectured me about . (something I did)......

When I had to ..... (something I did not want to do).. in front of everyone;

When to avoid trouble I had to (something I didn't want to do)

When I tried by doing... (something I did to help).. and it went wrong and I got blamed.

Often the trigger occurs when something that I wanted or expected didn't happen.

When I was left alone by ...... (name of person)...

When no one even noticed what I had done to help;

When .... (name of person)....ignored me;

A trigger can also be something that reminds me of unhappy past events.

When I hear .... on the radio;

When .... (name of person).... (who I love) is in pain;

When I smell the aroma of ....;

When .... (name of person).....is very needy and I feel I have to help by doing ... (something I do not want to do)....

Sometimes a trigger is a positive event but it feels so uncomfortable it causes a triggered reaction:

When .... (name of person).... complemented me about .. (something I did really well) ..... ;

Automatic F reaction patterns

Trigger events (usually or always) ignite your immediate, strong and *automatic* reaction or bring on feelings of extreme pain, discomfort, fear, confusion, disappointment or devastation, terror, panic, running, hiding, total surrender, freezing, overwhelming feelings of vulnerability or worthlessness, or just a deep sense of emotional pain.

Most people have a variety of over-reactions when they are triggered, depending on the situation, the people involved and the particular core belief that has been triggered.

For example:

I got angry and yelled at him /her.

I started to cry.

I hit him;

I got drunk.

I lied.

I panicked.

I 'got even'.

I sabotaged everything.

I went very quiet and didn't say a word.
I said things to her that I knew would make her go away.
I told ... what I thought she/he wanted to hear.
I criticised (or attacked) him / her.. about his/her faults.

Triggered Reactions follow a repetitive pattern

These are called Triggered or 'F' reactions and if they are repeated regularly they are described as triggered or F reaction ***patterns,*** as in the examples below.

Noticing and naming your triggers and then your repetitive reaction patterns are two of the keys which in turn help you discover your own old core beliefs.

However, whatever happens after you are triggered is not just a reaction.

What happens next is trying to protect you from your core pain and your underlying vulnerability, because you have just been "hot wired" back to that pain. It's intention is to reduce that emotional pain and so help you cope better. This is the immediate purpose behind most of your 'F' reaction patterns.

Reacting to Your own special triggers

For any one particular triggering event, as you experience it, you'll have a reaction. You may start fighting or fleeing, or instead fold into compliant surrender. Some reactions are like an explosion and very intense (*cannons*).

Some trigger a sense of being in a drama in which you are totally and unjustly '*crucified*'. Some reactions are cold, controlled and logical as if you brought in a large truckload of ready-mixed *concrete* and poured it over the problem (shutting down).

Some involve over playing a positive personality *characteristic* such as 'super happy'. Whichever one it might be, it is a sign that some of your younger inner selves have automatically taken control and are trying to 'manage' your reaction for you in the way (usually your PYRO teams) they think is best.

There's a better way to protect yourself

You will still get triggered in thew future, but as a grown up, you learn that that old kind of automatic reaction is not as effective as taking a more conscious approach to deal with your emotional, physical and mental responses when you are triggered.

That means you can choose whether to follow the same old mechanical automatic response pattern (F reaction) or choose a more aware way of dealing with the problem.

Typical Triggered or 'F' reactions

1. Fight or force
   (Trying to make other people change)
   - Firing from the hip or Flare up
   - Full on attack, Furious
   - Foot to the floor, Fanatic
   - Fix it Fast
   - Extreme envy or jealousy
2. Flee to get free Departing Deserting Escaping
   (Trying to get away from my Neg Core Belief)
3. Fold, Fling or Flog or Fawn
   (Trying to avoid conflict. Self defeating)
   - Fold and stay, over compliant Fawning
   - 'Fesssing up when you don't need to
   - Hurl or Fling it away, cynical, self sabotage
   - Flogging myself
4. Fearful Frightened Faint or Frozen
   (Overwhelmed by my Negative Core belief)
   - Freeze frame (stuck)
   - Floods of tears
   - Fragile Flower
   - Fatigued, too tired to do anything about it
5. Forceful Reasoning
   (Trying to resolve my Core issues using reason and logic)
   - Firmly Fixed (blocking change)
   - Stern Cold Logical Parent
   - Fair exchange
   - Fed up or Frightfully frustrated
   - Fixer Extraordinaire
6. Forget it
   (Helps me avoid or deny my Core Belief problems)
   - Fine all fixed
   - Walls of words (Filibuster)
7. Faulty Filters
   (Confusing myself while blaming others helps to maintain my belief)
   - Forecasting Future Failure
   - Frustratingly perverse
   - Fake it, Fool 'em and Fib
   - Flaws galore Versions 1, 2 and 3 (fault finding)
   - Exaggerating or Over Dramatising
   - Emotional Football
   - Fuzzy logic
   - Negative Judgements

Learning to recognise your triggers and your repetitive reaction "F" patterns gives you more awareness of which of your inner selves are at work, which helps you cope better with being triggered.

It also helps you get to know which particular inner selves most often take over in response to whatever triggers you.

This in turn helps you to recognise your core pain, your core issue and to understand the negative beliefs you have had about yourself.

Knowing and naming your reaction patterns

Before you can start to balance or moderate your protector reaction patterns you need to be familiar with them.

A repeated pattern means that the same protector system in you, a sub-personality or inner self is being kept busy protecting you from the same core pain that is connected to your old negative core belief.

When you complete Activity sheets CB-2, CB-4a and CB-4b and then CB-5 you'll be able to identify your own most common triggers as well as your reactions to them.

Each time you are triggered into an intense reaction, it's another chance to:

* acknowledge your real or core pain, allow yourself to feel it and to understand where it is really coming from (becoming authentic)
* discover more about your negative core beliefs, how they are controlling your life (even though they are no longer true) and how they stop you learning to deal with your core pain
* discover more about your automatic protector system (your inner selves) and what it can cost you when you allow an automatic set up to run your day for you
* try some new or different responses that you as a grown up aware self choose for yourself (manual override replacing automatic)

What is NOT a Triggered F reaction?

Not all reactions are triggered reactions. Many are just normal responses of the kind people around you would expect.

It is not likely to be a triggered F reaction if:

1. The power behind your response is at around the level most people would expect from anyone else in a similar situation. To other people, your response to that particular event would not appear to be amplified or inappropriate.
2. Your response reflects the reality of the situation. It doesn't project a distortion or exaggeration of the situation.
3. Your response is not an over-reaction but an authentic expression of your strong disapproval or dislike about something that has been said or done.
4. You are not shooting yourself in the foot by reacting this way. There is no sign that your reaction will end up in the long run doing ***you*** more harm than good as would F reactions such as *"Hurl or Fling it away"* or *"Firing from the Hip".*
5. Your reaction is more about *you as the person having the reaction*, as for example *"I feel so angry"* rather than projected outwards towards others as for example *"You make me so angry."*
6. This particular response or reaction is unique. It is not one of your 'too often repeated' response patterns. It is intentional, deliberate one-off not an automatic pattern.

Step 3
Signs of a core belief at work

Aim: Getting ready to make a list of some of your own more obvious behaviour patterns. That list will help you notice when you are hot wired to your own individual core belief.

It's time to look at some of the different problems that unbalanced core beliefs can create in your life.

Most "F" reaction patterns are intense and use up a lot of energy

Cannons, crucifixes, concrete and character

One of the more obvious signs that a core belief has been triggered is a noticeable shift in energy levels. Intense "F" over-reactions are usually directed outwards towards other people, the people we are hoping will help us fix our negative core belief.

They may be intended to pressure someone to stop doing what you don't want them to do to you. Or it may be your way of trying to make them say or do something that *(or so you believe)* should make you feel better about yourself.

There are many different kinds of over-reaction.

Cannons

For example, if the core belief is about not having enough power or control the visible response might be a rapid rise in the tone of voice or a highly energised body reaction (Examples: fighting, flaring or firing from the hip).

These energies are like *cannons* being fired at other people. As with real cannons the result is usually more damage and more war rather than more peace. Similar reactions that are designed to hide feelings of powerlessness are described as "revving the engine".

Crucifixes

If the core belief involves feelings such as guilt, shame or powerlessness the energy can still be intense and highly emotional, designed to gain support or sympathy from onlookers or watching audiences.

Projecting the speaker as an undeserving victim (like a martyr stuck on a *crucifix*) is somehow supposed to stop people doing what we don't want, or make them say words we need to hear so we will feel better inside.

At the same time tyour younger protector parts are trying to gain sympathy or support from 'outside' to help them deal with life's problems.

Concrete

Some reactions are intense but hidden. The intensity is focused inwards helping to hide or block feelings of vulnerability, escape reality or hide feelings from onlookers or audiences. Bottling up a strong emotion inside you can use up even more energy than other reactions as loads of rapid setting emotional *concrete* are poured over the issue to block the emotions inside. Mixing and pouring rapid setting emotional *concrete* is hard work.

Character (fake)

Some reactions involve over playing a 'fake' personality, as if following a script or acting a role on stage while wearing a mask. Example: pretending to be a very positive *character* and acting out the role of 'super happy' when this isn't authentic. That too takes lots of energy.

To remind yourself of these four different and very powerful over-reactions keep in mind the words, *cannons, crucifixes, concrete or character.*

At the heart of every core belief sits an underlying belief *"Who I am and how much I matter in the World is decided not by me but by people around me."* This is not true and as soon as you start questioning this you start escaping from your old core beliefs.

Notice how closely clue three, your Predictions and Expectations are connected to thoughts about how your underlying authentic sense of "...who I am" is undermined by thinking too much about "...what other people will think about me or what I expect they are going to do to me".

Activity Sheet - CB-2

Your Triggered Over- Reactions

Keep this sheet private - Show it only to your therapist or counsellor or to close friends who will respect your confidentiality

Work fast. Do not spend a lot of time on any one reaction. Only score the ones you do more often. If you feel your score on (a) and (b) are BOTH on the grey 1 to 4 side then do not score that reaction - record a zero total. But, if you feel your score on EITHER (a) or (b) is on the red 5 to 10 side just pick one number somewhere between 5 and 10 you think or feel might indicate how each (a) and (b) statement applies to you at present. Accurate scoring is not necessary. Wondering whether 6 or 7? - 8 or 9? Either one will give the same results.

Date _ _/_ _/_ _

1. Fighting or Forcing other people *Usually this is about trying to pressure other people change* Firing from the hip or Flare Up, Full on attack, Furious, Foot to the floor, Fanatic, Frightfully frustrated, Extreme envy or jealousy.

R1. Fight or force **- How often do I react this way?**

(a) Never 0_ 1_ 2_ 3_ 4 _5_ 6_7_ 8_ 9_10 Almost always

Usually, if or when I react this way, how intense are my feelings, my words or my tone of voice ?

(b) Very weak 0_ 1_ 2_ 3_ 4 _5_ 6_7_ 8_ 9_10 Very strong

My total Score for (a) and (b) R1 _ _ _ _

2. Fleeing Just to get free Departing Deserting Escaping *Trying to get away from my old Core Belief*

R2. Flee to get Free **- How often do I react this way?**

(a) Never 0_ 1_ 2_ 3_ 4 _5_ 6_7_ 8_ 9_10 Almost always

Usually, if or when I react this way, how intense are my feelings, my words or my tone of voice ?

(b) Very weak 0_ 1_ 2_ 3_ 4 _5_ 6_7_ 8_ 9_10 Very strong

My total Score for (a) and (b) R2 _ _ _ _

3. Fold Fawn Fling or Flog *Trying to avoid conflict. Usually Self defeating. Examples:* Fold and stay, Over compliant, Fawning, 'Fessing up; Hurl or Fling it away, Destructive self sabotage, Flogging myself.

R3. Folding Flinging or Flogging myself **- How often do I react this way?**

(a) Never 0_ 1_ 2_ 3_ 4 _5_ 6_7_ 8_ 9_10 Almost always

Usually, if or when I react this way, how intense are my feelings, my words or my tone of voice ?

(b) Very weak 0_ 1_ 2_ 3_ 4 _5_ 6_7_ 8_ 9_10 Very strong

My total Score for (a) and (b) R3 _ _ _ _

4. I feel Fearful Frightened Faint or Just Frozen *(Overwhelmed by my Negative Core belief)* Frozen (stuck) can't move; Floods of tears, Fragile Flower, Fatigued, Just too tired to do anything about it.

R4. I feel Fearful Frightened Faint or Frozen **- How often do I react this way?**

(a) Never 0_ 1_ 2_ 3_ 4 _5_ 6_7_ 8_ 9_10 Almost always

Usually, if or when I react this way, how intense are my feelings, my words or my tone of voice ?

(b) Very weak 0_ 1_ 2_ 3_ 4 _5_ 6_7_ 8_ 9_10 Very strong

My total Score for (a) and (b) R4 _ _ _ _

5. I use Forceful arguments *(Trying to resolve my Core issues using argument rather than calm reason or logic)* Firmly Fixed (argument based reasoning helps block my feelings); Firm Cold Logical parent, Fair exchange, Fixer Extraordinaire. *Explained in detail in Book CBal - 2*

R5. I use Forceful but not always Logical arguments **- How often do I react this way?**

(a) Never 0_ 1_ 2_ 3_ 4 _5_ 6_7_ 8_ 9_10 Almost always

Usually, if or when I react this way, how intense are my feelings, my words or my tone of voice ?

(b) Very weak 0_ 1_ 2_ 3_ 4 _5_ 6_7_ 8_ 9_10 Very strong

My total Score for (a) and (b) R5 _ _ _ _

6. Forget it *(Thinking hard helps me avoid or deny my Core Belief problems)* Fine all fixed; Walls of Words

R6 . Forget it **- How often do I react this way?**

(a) Never 0_ 1_ 2_ 3_ 4 _5_ 6_7_ 8_ 9_10 Almost always

Usually, if or when I react this way, how intense are my feelings, my words or my tone of voice ?

(b) Very weak 0_ 1_ 2_ 3_ 4 _5_ 6_7_ 8_ 9_10 Very strong

My total Score for (a) and (b) R6 _ _ _ _

7. Faulty Filters *(Confusing myself while blaming others helps to maintain my belief)* Forecasting Future Failure; Frustratingly perverse, Fake it, Fool 'em and Fib if I have to; Flaws galore Versions 1, 2 and 3 (excessive fault finding), Emotional Football, Exaggerating or Over Dramatising, Fuzzy logic, Negative Judgments.

R7 . Confusing myself and others **- How often do I react this way?**

(a) Never 0_ 1_ 2_ 3_ 4 _5_ 6_7_ 8_ 9_10 Almost always

Usually, if or when I react this way, how intense are my feelings, my words or my tone of voice ?

(b) Very weak 0_ 1_ 2_ 3_ 4 _5_ 6_7_ 8_ 9_10 Very strong

My total Score for (a) and (b) R7 _ _ _ _

If you feel you would like a more detailed explanation for any of these over reactions go to Book CBal - 2

Activity Sheet CB-3 (a)

Keep this sheet private - Show it only to your coach or counsellor or to close friends who will respect your confidentiality

Date _ _/_ _/_ _

What is a trigger? (Please read this first)

A trigger *is anything that regularly ignites immediate and strong reactions inside you* for example: a phrase, a specific comment, an action by another person. It can be a particular sight or sound. Another person's fear, pain or anger is often a trigger. A trigger can just as easily be anything you hoped for which did not happen.

1. When I am triggered ....

What kind of comments by others, what specific events or actions, what situations, sounds or tone of voice, what kind of touch, or emotion, what kind of music or even what smell can trigger a reaction like these in you?

Below, try to describe some of these specific events. Avoid general or vague examples such as *When I am blamed for losing things*. A better example: *'When Kim blamed me for losing the money'*. Try to include events from throughout your life starting with recent ones and working back in time.

Suggestions: *When ... said .. to me; When ... criticised me; When to prevent a fight I had to .....; When ... ignored me; When ... made me ...; When I was left all alone by ...; When .... (who I love) is in pain. When no one even noticed me. When ... complemented me about ..; When ... yelled at me and lectured me about ... When I had to ...... in front of everyone ..; When .... told me I was .....; When I hear ... playing on the radio; When I smell the aroma of ...; When .. was so unfair about ..;When I was forced to ...*

Then I imagined:

In this column, write what you *then* imagined about YOU or what you told yourself about who you are or are not, or what you predicted might happen to you? For example:

I imagined ..... that I was going to get hurt again; I knew I wasn't important; I told myself it was all my fault; that I didn't matter

(These are just some of the thoughts that can 'hot wire' you straight into your most common F reactions)

1. WHEN

2. WHEN

3. WHEN

4. WHEN

5. WHEN

6. WHEN
(for this one perhaps go back a few years)

7. WHEN
(for this one perhaps go back to a past relationship)

8. WHEN
(for this one perhaps go back to your teen years)

9. WHEN
(for this one perhaps go back to your childhood)

10. WHEN
(one more, that you remember from any time period)

Activity Sheet CB-3 (b)

Keep this sheet private - Show it only to your coach or counsellor or to close friends who will respect your confidentiality

Date _ _ _/ _ _ / _ _

Then I **felt** ...

In this column, write what you then felt: *Examples: Hurt, Sad, Pain, Panic, Fear, Alone, Guilt, Shame, Panic, Embarrassed, Confused, Frustrated, Angry, Anxious, Terrified, Devastated, Annoyed; Worthless*

(These are just some of the feelings that switch on your F reactions)

This is how I reacted or responded (my "F" reaction patterns)

After you are triggered, what do you do *automatically* (usually instantly)? *Noticing and naming your triggers and then your repetitive reaction patterns are two of the best clues that in turn help you discover your own unbalanced core beliefs. If you need to go back to Activity sheets CBal -1 to Cbal-3*

Examples: *I got angry and yelled at .. I went very quiet and didn't say a word. I started to cry. I said things to ...that I knew would make them go away. I panicked. Floods of tears. I told ... what I thought she/he wanted to hear. I went very calm and logical and tried to explain. I tried to control him/her. I criticised (or attacked) .. about his/her faults. I smiled and made a joke about it. I felt cold and started to shake. I wanted to run away and hide. I hit him; I got drunk. I lied. I tried to think positive thoughts. I tried to do exactly what he wanted. I 'got even'. I sabotaged everything.*

You can work on these four columns at random or in any order.

You might start with this one (Column 4) and work back to Col 1 or begin with Col 3 (feelings) and work both ways

Activity Sheet CB-4

Keep this sheet private - Show it only to your therapist or counsellor or to close friends who will respect your confidentiality

Date ___/___/___

What triggers my over-reactions? Summary

Looking back over what you have done so far what do you think might be your most common triggers, some of the words, actions, sounds, events (or anything else) that impact or trigger you? In particular look at your highest scores (page 39) and what you have written in your Activity Sheets

Some of my most common triggers are:

WHEN ____

____

WHEN ____

____

WHEN I ____

____

WHEN SOMEBODY ____

____

IF SOMEBODY ____

____

WHEN ___ *(something I want)* ___ doesn't happen ____________________________

____

WHEN ___ *(something I don't want)* ___ does happen ____________________________

____

MORE OF MY MOST COMMON TRIGGERS ____________________________

____

____

Activity Sheet CB-5

Keep this sheet private - Show it only to your therapist or counsellor or to close friends who will respect your confidentiality

Summary and Scores - Triggered Over-Reactions

Date _ _ _/ _ _ / _ _

These Activity sheets have helped you focus on the most common ways how you, just like other people, are being impacted by your unbalanced core beliefs. The higher your total scores the more likely that one or more of your unbalanced core beliefs is involved.

My Total for sheet CB-1_ _ _ _ _ (page 25)

My Total for Reactions R1 _ _ _ _ _ (page 32)

My Total for Reactions R2 _ _ _ _ _ (page 32)

My Total for Reactions R3 _ _ _ _ (page 32)

My Total for Reactions R4 _ _ _ _ (page 32)

My Total for Reactions R5 _ _ _ _ (page 32)

My Total for Reactions R6 _ _ _ _ (page 32)

My Total for Reactions R7 _ _ _ _ (page 32)

1. Out of all my reactions (R1 to R7 (page 32) **my three highest scoring or most common 'F' reaction patterns** (from the R groups above) **are:**

R _ _ _ _ _ _ _ _ (words) _ _ _ _ _ _ _ _ _ _ _

_ _ _ _ _ _ _ _ _ _ _ _ _ _ _ _ _ _ Score _ _ _ _

R _ _ _ _ _ _ _ _ (words) _ _ _ _ _ _ _ _ _ _ _

_ _ _ _ _ _ _ _ _ _ _ _ _ _ _ _ _ _ Score _ _ _ _

R _ _ _ _ _ _ _ _ (words) _ _ _ _ _ _ _ _ _ _ _

_ _ _ _ _ _ _ _ _ _ _ _ _ _ _ _ _ _ Score _ _ _ _

2. Out of all my reactions (R1 to R7 (page 32) **my next highest scoring or next most common 'F' reaction patterns (from the groups above) are:**

R. _ _ _ _ _ _ (words) _ _ _ _ _ _ _ _ Score _ _ _ _

R. _ _ _ _ _ _ (words) _ _ _ _ _ _ _ _ Score _ _ _ _

R. _ _ _ _ _ _ (words) _ _ _ _ _ _ _ _ Score _ _ _ _

3. Look back over your most familiar "F" over-reactions. When you react in these ways what might you also be trying to get other people to do or say or think that could help you feel better about yourself?

_ _

_ _

. _

4. Look back over your most familiar "F" over-reactions. What do you tell yourself or believe about yourself that might be connected with your regular choice of those particular F reaction patterns?

_ _

_ _

. _

Scoring your results for Activity sheets CB-1 and CB-2

Sheet CB-1 0-65 Limited core Belief; 66-70 Yes you have one; 71-90 and it's biting;

Reactions R1 4-5 Caution; 6-10 Few problems, 11-15 Expect problems; 16+ Too strong High risk PYRO*

Reactions R2 4-5 Caution; 6-8 Few problems, 9-15 Expect problems; 16+ Escaping too much

Reactions R3 4-5 Caution; 6-10 Few problems, 9-15 Expect problems; 16+ Too disempowering

Reactions R4 4-5 Caution; 6-10 Few problems, 11-15 Expect problems; 16+ Disempowering risks

Reactions R5 4-5 Caution; 6-10 Few problems, 1 1-15 Expect problems; 16+ Too strong

Reactions R6 4-5 Caution; 6-10 Few problems, 11-15 Expect problems; 1 6+ Wasted energy

Reactions R7 4-5 Caution; 6-10 Few problems, 11-15 Expect problems; 16+ Is your PYRO* team still driving your bus?

* Terms such as PYRO are codes to help identify the different emotional ages we all go through every day.
All emotional ages normal. but some work better than others depending on the situation.
They are explained in detail on pages 111 -114 at the end of this book

Clue Number Two

Whenever you try too hard to get another person to help reduce your pain or treat you in a better way - that's your ....

Disempowering Belief that drives your 'Outside of Me' or 'Give me' Intention

Your triggered or F reactions are whatever you automatically do or say moments after you have been triggered or hot wired to your Core Belief. However what you do after you are triggered is not just a reaction. It is intended in some way to protect you from your core pain and your underlying vulnerability, to reduce your emotional pain and so help you cope better.

However, there are two more underlying intentions behind your reactions.

* To hide your core pain from other people.

* To get another person to do something to help reduce your pain or to have them treat you in a better way.

These are your "outside of me" intentions.

Those extra two intentions are what Nikki Nemerouf describes as your automatic intentions. I prefer to describe them as your "Outside of Me or Give me " intentions based on a false belief:

"Most power is outside of me" It's held by other people (false)

Your Outside of Me or Give me Intention

An example of an Outside of Me Intention might be to try to get a 'better' answer from another person about who they think you are or what they think about you. The intention is based on the feeling that it must help you if you can get other people to say those 'right' words (the words you so much want to hear). Or it may be to get them to do the 'right' thing (that you so much want them to do) or make something happen (that you want to happen so much to help reduce your core pain.)

I agree with Nikki Nemerouf that these 'outside of me' intentions just like your F reactions are largely automatic and seldom conscious.

But can you sse the paradox of a protection system that is trying to get someone else to help ease your hurting at the same time as it is trying to hide that pain from them!

Notice also, the problems of having a mechanism trying to ease your pain automatically, which means you have no awareness of its operation, no conscious control over it and no choice about what it does?

Second Clue

Unmasking The Disempowering Belief behind every Core Belief

"Life is on top of me. Life holds all the real power. I don't."

This over-riding belief, sadly, *might have been true* when you were a child. *IT IS NOT TRUE TODAY* but if you continue to believe it you'll have trouble locating your powerful positive belief which is *inside you*, not outside.

What do you do next

To resolve this you first needed to become more aware of your most familiar over-reactions. That was your first clue. Your second clue is to identify your 'Outside of Me ot Give me Intentions' that operate alongside those reactions.

This awareness needs to operate very quickly, ideally at the same moment your automatic reaction is trying to take over, rather than afterwards.

One way of speeding up identification of your automatic ".... what do I want other people to do for me?" intention is to have made a list in advance of your most common patterns, particularly the ones that you have already noticed contain a strong "outside of me or give me" content.

Look for a common factor or repeated theme in the type of energy involved. An energy pattern such as over active compensating skills or too many overwhelmed emotionally young inner selves telling you that you 'have to' do things are common examples.

Most people have a variety of outside of me intention patterns depending on the situation, the kind of core pain or negative belief and of course who else is involved.

What issues that seem to be outside you are really inside you?

Can you start to see how often you have tried to hide all this from other people and yet at the same time wanted them to change to help you feel better about yourself.

Trying to get others to change so you'll feel better about your belief is a waste of your time and theirs too.

Use Activity sheets CB- 6 CB-7 and CB- 8 to highlight what you might have been trying to hide from other people and what you might have been trying to get from other people in order to have them to help you deal with *your old core belief.*

Your old unbalanced core beliefs tell you that who you are and how much you matter in the World is determined by other people, not by you. ***This is not true.***

What's behind Clue Number Two?

Who I am and How Much I matter is decided by Other People (false)

This False belief disempowers me and helps me give my power away, every day

Almost all our problems with old core beliefs are connected to, or driven by, the same one underlying (and untrue) belief - that who you are and how much you matter is determined by other people, not by you. *This is not true.*

Looking back over your first clue can you see now how this was connected to this same false belief. Almost every "F" reaction is aimed at getting somebody to do what we want or stop them doing what we don't want.

Example: I will feel much better inside, if I can just **make** people (outside of me) treat me better, care more about me or do what I want.

Almost every forecast, prediction or prophecy we make about what we believe somebody will or won't do for us and what will go wrong is driven by this same false belief.

Once you stop believing people have so much power over you, you won't get triggered as much and you won't have as many "F" reactions. You won't make as many predictions or forecasts about things that probably won't happen. You will still have your wonderful compensating skills but they will become a true gift that you share with others instead of a compensation.

The next two clues after this are also connected to the same false belief that *"Most power is held by other people and outside of me"*

This false belief creates big power problems

Each time you give your power away you are "disempowering" yourself and at the heart of almost every disempowering pattern there sits this same deeply felt, powerful yet false belief *(inside me)* that works hand in hand with a Core Belief:

This incredibly powerful false belief emphasises that " ... **the power is outside of me."** *(false).*

This leads to a number of disempowering beliefs and predictions. All are untrue.:

*** There is a person, a process, or an object *outside me* which is more powerful than me. *(false)***

and

*** This *outside of me* person, that substance, that object, that activity (any or all of them) are exactly what I need to *"make me"* feel loved, worthwhile, safe, good enough.** Only they, alone (or it alone) can fix my problems and at the same time take away my shame, heal my emotional wounding and stop my worrying or grieving or holding on to a sense of loss. *(false)*

*** They have the key, I don't. *(false)***

These disempowering beliefs are usually accompanied by supporting beliefs that this person, object or process possesses *the only key* that can unlock these longed for feelings and solve my problems. That person that object or that process has the power and the key. *(false)*

*** BUT .... If I can make them do that for me *then* I will feel much better inside. *(false)***

If a disempowering belief involves another *person*, then it will tell you that he or she holds some kind of magical power to fix things for you *"if only she or he wanted to"*. So if I have any power it will be in my ability to make them do this for me! *(false)* If I fail it proves again that I have no power. *(false)*

It's much the same with activities like gambling, work addiction or love addiction. If I can just put enough effort or time or money into the way I do that powerful activity then I can make that activity fix things inside me that I can't fix myself. *(false)*

If the magic thing is a substance, alcohol, nicotine, or food or a drug it's the same. If, after three drinks it's starting to show its magic power to fix things inside me, then I must have six drinks. That way I will make it work harder for me. *(false).*

The reality…. self-empowerment

The reality is that it is my job alone to fix things inside me by myself, especially all my sad, painful, not good enough feelings. Only I can fix those feelings.

Wanting others to feel my pain means I want them to help fix it for me. When I can feel it by myself, I can heal it by myself.

The measure of my own personal power is how often I can do this successfully, all by myself. Each time I do this I am closer to becoming the "real, the truly authentic, the really powerful me".

Where this old false belief comes from…..

It's understandable that as a child you would believe that you had to rely on people outside of you to get your needs met, fix your childhood problems, help you feel loved and happy inside and outside.

If this didn't happen for you as a child then this can set up an unfortunate level of reliance on finding another "outside of me person" or an activity to do the job you believed then that you could never do for yourself.

Often parents, teachers and older siblings all told you that you needed them to help you fix things. In return for their help you had to do what they wanted or even the be the person they wanted you to be.

This is why the old belief can continue to be so powerful because when you were a kid it made things easier if you believed it was true, did what other powerful people wanted and fitted in with their plans for you and your life.

Most F style over-reaction patterns have one common intention, to control other people, in the sense that we want to "make them" stop whatever they're doing that triggers us.
Yet we still feel surprised when other people feel controlled or they fight our control. That's <u>their</u> reaction or, in most cases, <u>their</u> over-reaction in response to <u>our</u> over reaction

The more I want somebody else to feel my pain the more it means I want them to heal my pain.
The more I can feel it by myself the more I can heal it by myself

This can lead to another disempowering and false belief about your future.

* I will never be permitted to be the "real me". **I don't have the power within me to be that wonderful, special "me" that I want to be.**

(false)

Can you start to see now how often you have tried to hide all this from other people and yet at the same time wanted them to change to help you feel better about yourself.

Trying to get others to change so you'll feel better about your belief is a waste of your time and theirs too.

Use Activity sheets CB- 6 CB-7 and CB- 8 to highlight what you might have been trying to hide from other people and what you might have been trying to get from other people in order to have them to help you deal with *your old core belief.*

Activity Sheet CB- 6

Keep this sheet private - Show it only to your therapist or counsellor or to close friends who will respect your confidentiality

Second Clue - Your Disempowering Belief

Date __/__/__

"Most power is held by other people and outside of me" - Part A

Your unbalanced core beliefs tell you that who you are and how much you matter is determined by other people, not by you. This is untrue. When you are triggered, your core beliefs usually tell you that you must then look to the person who triggered you to help relieve your pain or to make things better for you.

A. In what ways do people treat you that you find hurts you the most? Example: 'People ignore me'.

B. What is it that other people <u>don't do</u> for you that hurts you most? Example: 'People don't listen to me'.

My "Outside of me or Give me" intentions:

What do I want other people to give me because I know that would help me feel better about myself (their approval, respect, peace, love, physical gifts, sex, love, power, etc. etc.

What is it I want those people to say or do that would help me feel better about the feelings I have inside me.

What I would like other people to change about themselves that would help me feel better about myself

Examples:

I may be afraid to ask but I want them to give me their:

approval, agreement, attention, time, encouragement, praise, respect, peace, love, physical gifts, sex, love, power, joy

I want them to stop:

criticising me, judging me, getting angry, crying

I want them to change their:

feelings, words, appearance, tone of voice, clothing, hair, friends

Of those requests that I make (asking others to change themselves to help me, feel better) which of my requests would help me most to feel better about myself?

You can keep on doing this, but you'll almost always fail to get what you hoped from them, or feel any better.

How successful am I at getting these things to happen?

Activity Sheet CB- 7

Keep this sheet private - Show it only to your therapist or counsellor or to close friends who will respect your confidentiality

Second Clue

Date __/__/__

Most power is held by other people and outside of me" - Part B

Work fast. Do not spend a lot of time on any one item. Only score the ones you do more often. *If you feel your score on any line is between 1 to 4 then score a zero. But, if you feel your score is on the* red 5 to 10 side *just pick one number somewhere between 5 and 10 that you think or feel might indicate how each statement applies to you* *__at present__.*

1.1 There is something I do not want to happen or something I do not want someone to say or do to me. But it still seems to happen to me quite often and suddenly I feel a sharp sense inside me of emotional pain, negative thoughts or feelings about who I am, or who I am not. What are your strongest thoughts or feelings when this happens. This list might help: _ _ _ _ _ _ _ _ _ _ _ _ _ _ _

_ _

_ _

If your thoughts or feelings are not included in the list on the right please add your own.

At that moment how powerful are those thoughts or feelings inside me?
Very weak 0_ 1_ 2_ 3_ 4 _5_ 6_7_ 8_ 9_10 *Very powerful effect on me*

Events like this and thoughts or feelings like this occur in my life
Hardly ever 0_ 1_ 2_ 3_ 4 _5_ 6_7_ 8_ 9_10 *Almost all the time*

I can't help feeling deep down inside that this keeps happening to me:
I have no idea why 0_ 1_ 2_ 3_ 4 _5_ 6_7_ 8_ 9_10 *Because I am just not good enough*

1.2. There was something that I hoped for or really wanted to happen, or something I really hoped someone would say or do and nothing happened. Quite suddely I feel a sharp sense inside me of emotional pain, negative thoughts or feelings about who I am, or who I am not, What are your strongest thoughts or feelings when this happens. This list might help: _ _ _ _ _ _ _ _ _ _ _ _ _ _ _

_ _

_ _

If your thoughts or feelings are not ncluded in the list on the right please add your own.

At that moment how powerful were those thoughts or feelings inside me?
Very weak 0_ 1_ 2_ 3_ 4 _5_ 6_7_ 8_ 9_10 *Very powerful effect on me*

Events like this and thoughts or feelings like this occur my life
Hardly ever 0_ 1_ 2_ 3_ 4 _5_ 6_7_ 8_ 9_10 *Almost all the time*

I can't help feeling deep down inside that this keeps happening to me:
I have no idea why 0_ 1_ 2_ 3_ 4 _5_ 6_7_ 8_ 9_10 *Because I am just not good enough*

1.3. Think of a couple of other things that happen to you when suddenly once again you feel that sharp sense inside of emotional pain, negative thoughts or feelings. What are your strongest thoughts or feelings when this happens. This list might help:

_ _

_ _

If your thoughts or feelings are not included in the list on the right please add your own..

At that moment how powerful were those thoughts or feelings inside me?
Very weak 0_ 1_ 2_ 3_ 4 _5_ 6_7_ 8_ 9_10 *Very powerful effect on me*

Events like this and thoughts or feelings like this occur in my life
Hardly ever 0_ 1_ 2_ 3_ 4 _5_ 6_7_ 8_ 9_10 *Almost all the time*

I can't help feeling deep down inside that this keeps happening to me:
I have no idea why 0_ 1_ 2_ 3_ 4 _5_ 6_7_ 8_ 9_10 *Because I am just not good enough*

My total for the nine questions above ______

I feel a I am just not good I'm not lovable; I can't make it work, I'm always wrong; I'm un-balanced, I have no value, I am powerless. It's all my fault.

I feel intense feelings inside me like: Pain, Anger, Rage, Fighting, Doubt, Blamed, Guilty, Ashamed, Hurt, Sadness, Grief, Fear, Jealousy, Envy, Victim, Worried, Alone, Panic, Unsafe, Loss, Lost, Embarrassment, Confused, Controlled, Frustrated, Offended, Terrified, Trapped, Smothered, Devastated, Annoyed; Manipulated, Worthless;

I keep doing things again and again like:

Fighting, Arguing, Resisting, Running away, Controlling, Blaming, I keep shooting myself in the foot

Activity Sheet CB- 8

Keep this sheet private - Show it only to your therapist or counsellor or to close friends who will respect your confidentiality

Second Clue

Date __/__/__

Who I am and How Much I matter is decided by Other People (false)

Work fast. Do not spend a lot of time on any one reaction. Only score the ones you do more often. If you feel your score on any line is between 1 to 4 then score a zero. But, if you feel your score is on the red 5 to 10 side just pick one number somewhere between 5 and 10 that you think or feel might indicate how each statement applies to you at present. Accurate scoring is not necessary.

What do you feel, expect or predict from people around you?

2.1 Think back to the previous activity sheet. Someone says or does something to you or just as often something that you hoped for or wanted does not happen. Or someone does not say or do something you hoped for. These events are your **"triggers"**. You know you have been triggered because you feel that sharp sense inside you of emotional pain accompanied by whatever thoughts or feelings are most common for you whenever this happens.
This time think about the other person and about your wishes or feelings in regard to that person at the time when they triggered you.

How much do I feel they are responsible for triggering me and making me feel that way?

They are not at all responsible 0_ 1_ 2_ 3_ 4 _5_ 6_7_ 8_ 9_10 They are totally responsible

How much effort did I put into trying to stop them triggering me again, getting them to help fix the problem, or trying to get a 'better' response from them?

Very little effort 0_ 1_ 2_ 3_ 4 _5_ 6_7_ 8_ 9_10 I tried everything I could

How successful was I? Did I get them to do what I wanted?

Very successful 0_ 1_ 2_ 3_ 4 _5_ 6_7_ 8_ 9_10 No success at all

2.2. What are some of the things you expect, predict or tell yourself other people are likely to do to you again and again and that are likely to trigger you? Examples: "People won't like me. "People don't trust me". "Even my friends think I am stupid" "I will get hurt or ripped off" "Everyone ignores me" "I will lose this one" "Nobody will help me" "Nobody likes me".

_ _

_ _

_ _

As I write these forecasts how strong are my negative feelings about these people?

Very weak 0_ 1_ 2_ 3_ 4 _5_ 6_7_ 8_ 9_10 Very strong

How often do I find my forecasts about these people turn out to be right?

Very seldom 0_ 1_ 2_ 3_ 4 _5_ 6_7_ 8_ 9_10 Almost all the time

2.3. Something good happens to a person you know well or you notice they are feeling delight, excitement, happiness or the joy of their success and quite suddenly you feel a sharp sense inside you of negative feelings like those on this list.

At that moment how strong are ***my negative feelings*** about them?

Very weak 0_ 1_ 2_ 3_ 4 _5_ 6_7_ 8_ 9_10 Strong negative feelings about them

Events like these and my reactions like these occur in my life

Hardly ever 0_ 1_ 2_ 3_ 4 _5_ 6_7_ 8_ 9_10 Very often

When I ask myself why this is happening to them, but not to me:

I have no idea why 0_ 1_ 2_ 3_ 4 _5_ 6_7_ 8_ 9_10 Because .... _ _ _ _ _ _

_ _

If your thoughts or feelings are not included in the list on the right please add your own.

My total for the nine questions above ______

I feel I am just not good enough; I'm not lovable; I can't make it work, I'm always wrong; I'm un-balanced, I have no value, I am powerless. It's all my fault.
I feel intense feelings inside me like:
Pain, Anger, Rage, Fighting, Doubt, Blamed, Guilty, Ashamed, Hurt, Sadness, Grief, Fear, Jealousy, Envy, Victim, Worried, Alone, Panic, Unsafe, Loss, Lost, Embarrassment, Confused, Controlled, Frustrated, Offended, Terrified, Trapped, Smothered, Devastated, Annoyed; Manipulated, Worthless;
I keep doing things again and again like:
Fighting, Arguing, Resisting, Running away, Controlling, Blaming,
I keep shooting myself in the foot

You are not 'your behaviour'

'I am who I am - not what I do'

He may have told you a lie but that lie does not turn him into a 'liar" as people often seem to believe. He is not 'his behaviour'.

An anti-labelling boundary

This is a good time to remember the so often forgotten wisdom that ***you are not your behaviour"*** or in Pia Mellody's words **... *"Your doings are not your beings."***

You may do or say something while you're angry but that does not mean to are being 'an angry person'. Yet we fall into this trap so often.

We have different 'being descriptions' to describe a person who shoots and kills someone. That person may be a police officer or a soldier. It could be a killer loose on the street. Who they are *being* at the time affects the way we see what they are *doing* in moral terms. But what they did does not define who they are.

Some people may judge a single woman who enjoys sex outside a committed relationship. She is being a single woman who chooses to be active sexually but if people do not approve of what she is doing they give her a 'being' label. She is a ......

A man who does the same thing will be given a different being label. He is a man but it is what he is doing that we notice and according to whether we approve or disapprove we may label him as being "a stud" or being "a ...."

In the box (next page) are some powerful spoken or written boundaries that help you reject negative generalising or labelling especially when people try to tell you who you are.

If the label don't fit, don't wear it. Reject a negative Inventory

If you find yourself on the receiving end of a long line of negative *"you are ..."* messages, delivered one after the other, that's a negative inventory. Usually the inventory is delivered face to face but sometimes it is done by letter, over the phone or by e-mail.

Flaws Galore

Here's an example of a typical one-way negative inventory that starts something like this and runs non-stop.

"You are ...."

"You never ...."

"You always ...."

"You think you are ...."

"You don't ...."

Usually it doesn't stop there.

Negative Inventory continued

"You can't ...."

"You won't ...."

"You make me feel sad ...."

"You make me so angry ...."

"You always hurt me ......"

"You're cruel ...."

"You're stupid!/ wrong / an idiot / dumb."

"You haven't got a clue!"

"You're crazy ...."

"You need .....(psychiatric)...... help!"

"You don't have the slightest ...."

"You're a loser ...."

"You just ...."

"You ...."

Block or reject these messages right at the very start

You need strong boundaries to make sure those rapidly repeated *'you are'* messages don't start to undermine you. That can happen so quickly.

Don't get tricked into using logic or reason or try to defend yourself. That's exactly what they want because then they can keep their negative inventory going.

Instead, establish your sense of total rejection *inside you*, by blocking their messages out completely and firmly right from the start.

As soon as you hear the first *'You are ..... '* start saying to yourself:

"Who I am and how much I matter in the World is none of their business."

If you can, and *if it's safe to do so*, then try telling the Negative Controlling person the same things using those lines and other lines in the box on the next page.

Memorising the phrases long before you need them is a good idea. Better still rehearse your lines just like an actor, saying them out loud, over and over.

Most F style over-reaction patterns have one common intention, to control other people, in the sense that we want to "make them" stop whatever they're doing that triggers us.

Yet we still feel surprised when they feel controlled or resisit our control. That's their counter reaction or, in most cases, their over-reaction

If the label don't fit, don't wear it!

"Because, who I am .... is none of Their business!"

...... Pia Mellody

Dealing with negative "You are ....." messages

When another person starts a sentence with:

"You are .... (any negative label) ...."

that's a good time to remind yourself:

1. It's only a label, it's their label, not yours. *And it's not even true.*
2. Who you are, and how much you matter in the World, is none of their business.
3. If the label don't fit, don't wear it. *It is your absolute right to reject their label (totally).* Tell 'em, it's their label. It isn''t yours, it doesn't fit you and you aren't wearing it, no matter how much they want you to.
4. Remind yourself. It's all about something they want you to do, say, think or feel for them. It's their 'give me' intention!

   Remind yourself this is only about something they want from you .... *I wonder what they want me to do, say, think or feel for them.* If it's safe, you might even ask, *"What is it you really want from me?"*
5. If they run three or more negative "you" label messages, one after the other, that's called a negative inventory. The more negative *"You" ....* messages all at the one time, the less they are true. If there is one negative thing that might be true about you, that will be the one they *don't mention* in their list.
6. If it's really about anything you do, or don't do, remember *what you do* is still NOT *who you are.*

WARNING This can also apply to similar kinds of:

"You are ..... (overly flattering or fake compliment type) ..... labels.

Third clue - Your Predictions Forecasts and Expectations

Aim: Alerting yourself to the power any core belief has to set up repeated self-fulfilling negative events in your life.

Look back at things that have occurred in your life again and again, repeated failures or fights or foul ups that have the same or similar patterns.

It wasn't just the universe picking you out for a repeated problem, it was actually a Core Belief based predictions and forecasts that helped set up these negative events (and encouraged the people who helped create the events!) into your life. After you balance a Core Belief this will stop.

Sheet CB-10 is light-hearted but behind it is the serious reminder of how we really do send messages like this out to the world and that's why people treat us in negative ways. After you balance your core beliefs this will stop.

At the heart of every core belief sits an underlying belief *"Who I am and how much I matter in the World is decided not by me but by people around me."* This is not true and as soon as you start questioning this you start escaping from your old core beliefs.

Notice how many old beliefs are connected to underlying thoughts of "...who I am" depends on "... what I have to do for them".

Progress Check - Steps 1 to 3

1. Where do unbalanced or negative core beliefs come from?

2. Are they good or bad?

3. Why not just get rid of them?

4. What are some of the most obvious signs that tell you an unbalanced core belief is 'at work' inside you or that you're "driving under the influence" of an unbalanced core belief?

5. What are some signs that tell you that you someone else who you know might also be "driving under the influence" of an unbalanced core belief?

You can't "think it through" But you can balance it.

Aim: Appreciate why sensible, rational analytical thinking will not (and cannot) lead you closer to discovering your core beliefs. Nor can thinking harder help reduce their effect on your life. Understand why *it is not easy* to recognise a Core Belief and why you cannot "think it through", or just put it into words.

But you can balance it.

This will also give you some idea of some of the tricks and traps ahead as you as you start looking more closely at your own F patterns.

Clue Number Three

Expectations, Predicting and Forecasting Beliefs

Self-fulfilling prophecies

Predictions, Forecasts and similar supporting beliefs help protect us from unpleasant surprises by making lots of predictions about how other people are going to treat us. In trying to prepare ourselves for predicted trouble we unconsciously do things that help make what we predicted happen, *just the way we expected.*

CORE BELIEF MAP

Your old core beliefs help you set up a 'map of your world' and then suggest what you must do or not do, to discover 'your place' in that world or 'fit in' with your family. According to the kind of core belief (balanced or unbalanced, negative or positive) the map you construct may, or may not, be accurate, *or it could be upside down.*

Everyone unconsciously constructs a belief system, a 'map of their world' which helps them to:

1. Prepare for what might happen to them in the future
2. Protect themselves from unexpected outcomes or reactions by other people
3. Interpret other people's motives and the meanings behind other people's actions in terms of *"It must be something about me that causes them to react that way."*

If your map is based on well balanced, accurate and positive beliefs then your predictions about the future should be fairly accurate.

However, if the map is based on unbalanced or negative beliefs, the forecasts, predictions and prophecies will also be negative, and inaccurate and will lead to misinterpretations, misunderstandings and self-fulfilling predictions.

The 'self-fulfilling prophecy'

The trouble is that what you do to stop the predicted problem almost always makes it more likely to happen. It's as if taking an umbrella increases the chance of a thunderstorm.

This is aptly described as a 'self-fulfilling prophecy', suggesting that what you expect or predict is more likely to happen *because of the things you do to prepare yourself for it.* This is even more likely whenever your predictions tell you 'it is going to happen again.'

Predicting a catastrophe.

Negative Predictions and other Supporting Beliefs can be responsible for some awfully bad forecasts about what is going to happen. ***In the most severe cases some people predict a total catastrophe not just a negative events.***

It's all your fault anyway

Your predictions, forecasts and expectations tell you there is a *direct connection* between your negative beliefs about yourself and what other people do to you (or what you think they will do).

These kinds of belief help you prepare yourself for how you expect you are going to be treated.

That may have helped you when, as a child, predict that somebody would harm you. That way you were not caught unawares.

Your forecasting and predicting beliefs along with your negative core beliefs helped you 'fit in' and so be less vulnerable. They helped you know what to expect and adjust your feelings in advance to cope better when it happened the next time.

Identifying Your Predicting or Forecasting beliefs

There is one easy way to distinguish a supporting belief from a core belief. Your core beliefs will always be statements about you. Two common examples are: *"I am powerless"; "I am not safe"*

On the other hand, your preditctions and forecasts will always be about what other people can be expected to do to you and which will hurt you or will cause you to have a strong triggered or F reaction?

Examples of supporting beliefs:

'People ignore me' or 'People don't listen to me'.

'Nobody likes / trusts/ believes / appreciates / cares about / me.

Everybody hates / dislikes / distrusts / me.

Your predictions and forecasts and expectations prepare you for future vulnerability, because they just know ***".... it's going to happen again!'*** So they help support your old core belief with 'weather forecasts':

Expectations and other supporting beliefs

Predicting and Preparing **-** for what to expect *from other people* - the way other people are going to act towards me - *'She won't like me ; He will leave me'* etc.

Prophecies or Forecasts **-** about what *is going to happen to me - 'I will always be alone. I'll never get it right. It will all go wrong again'* etc.

If your core beliefs are unbalanced and negative your expectations will be unbalanced and negative too

I can't trust other people. I must not trust people'. Other people always ...... me ;

Other people never .....like/trust/appreciate ..... me.

Supporting beliefs

But predictions and forecasts are not core beliefs. They are supporting beliefs because they support your core belief.

Your big red neon Sign

To add to the problem, whatever your unique negative beliefs about yourself might be, they will unconsciously attract (towards you) the kind of people whose behaviour fits in with your negative beliefs, as if you had a big red neon sign over your head inviting the very people who will trigger your core beliefs to come in and do just that!

At the same time your old beliefs will help you repel or distance yourself from positive people who don't fit in with your beliefs. And this in turn, will shape many of the ways those people then react towards you! In this way, core beliefs control many of the recurring event in your life. They influence major life decisions including your choice of a career and marriage partner, but unfortunately in a less than positive way.

In the end the predictions and forecasts and what we do to try to stop them coming true all get mixed up. Whether positive or negative, the core issue that you project will attract people into your life (and attract you to people) who will help 'prove' the truth of your old and false belief.

People who discover they have a core belief that they are so unlovable that they don't deserve a worthwhile partner are often amazed as they look back and notice how many partners they have had who each treated them like a doormat. (It is as if their neon sign only attracted that one kind of person.)

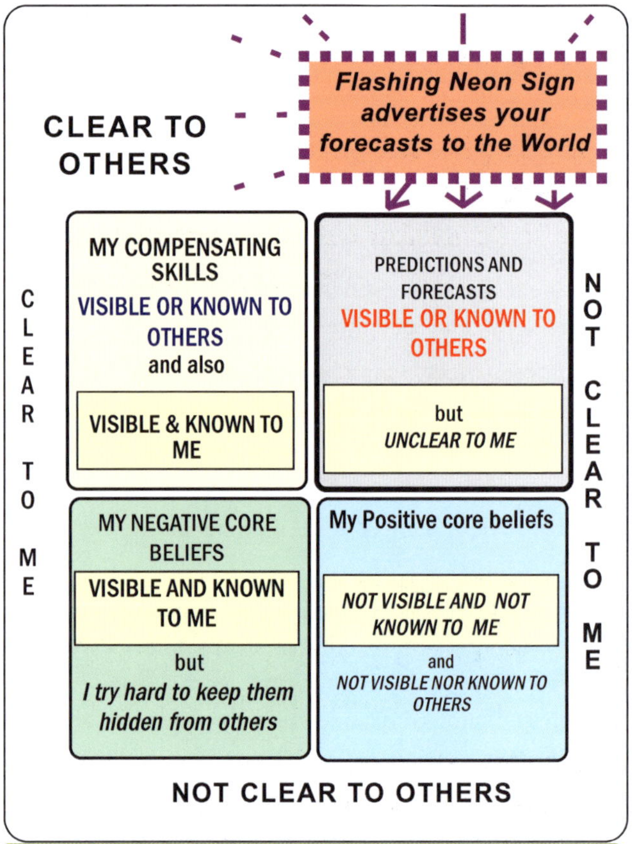

Acknowledgement: This diagram has been adapted from the well known "Jo Hari Window" with my appreciation to Joseph Luft and Harrington Ingham, who gifted it to the world in 1955

Taking an umbrella won't increase the chance of a thunderstorm. But our negative forecasts work that way!

Once you forecast a negative event and what you then do to try to stop it happening often has a direct and observable outcome. What you do *increases the chances that the negative event will occur.* People read your flashing red neon sign and they react accordingly but in the opposite way to what you wanted.

You can turn the sign off!

People are amazed to discover what happens after they balance an old belief with a positive one such as 'I am special and I deserve to share my life with another special person', the equivalent to turning off the old sign.

Suddenly they start meeting new kinds of people, and forming new relationships where their partners really value them and treat them as special.

Case study - Other People's Sparklers vs My Explosives

I'm driving down the road in my truck. On the back are several bales of dry hay, some explosives and two drums of high octane fuel which I'm taking home to put in my shed. I haven't bothered to cover the load.

You are standing at the side of the road, celebrating a promotion, a new relationship, a success and you're just so happy. You're waving sparklers (the ones that give off live sparks) to share your joy.

About a minute later my truck blows up. Luckily I survive but I remember seeing you waving those sparklers and immediately I blame you for "causing" the explosion and the loss of my truck.

We can all do this so easily, because it seems to help us if we can identify the "other person" as responsible for our triggers and our explosions.

We forget that carrying the explosive materials is 100% our responsibility and ours alone. We also forget it's us who did nothing to protect our load from passing sparks. (That's what our boundary system is supposed to do for us).

Examples of Disempowering Belief Patterns

False belief - Who I am and how much I matter is determined by other people, not by me.

False belief - blaming other people makes it harder for my old unbalanced Core belief to make me feel blamed.

False belief - If I scare or punish other people enough they will treat me much better and then I will feel better inside.

False belief - people will treat me better if I keep reminding them about how unfortunate I am.

False belief - I would feel much better inside, if I could just run fast enough to get away from people who remind me of my old Negative Core Belief.

False belief - I have only two choices about my personal power. Either I must fight like a tiger to hang on to it or I must give it all away.

False belief - I would feel much better inside, if I could solve all my Core issues using the magic power of reason and logic to get other people to care more about me.

True: Wanting others to feel my pain means I want them to help fix it for me. When I can feel it by myself, I can heal it by myself.

When you are triggered, your core beliefs usually tell you that you must then look to the person who triggered you to help relieve your pain.
You can keep on doing this, but you'll almost always fail to get what you hoped from them, or feel any better

Typical Predictions, Forecasts, Expectations and Self-fulfilling prophecies

Predicting or Forecasting based on our negative core beliefs are supposed to help protect us from unpleasant surprises. So we make lots of forecasts, predictions and prophecies about:

1. How other people are going to treat us
2. What we will have to do to get them to treat us better
3. Why the answer is outside of us and inside them
4. How we can only feel 'good enough' inside *after we get people to change* the way they treat us.

WARNING! If we react to a forecast based on a core belief our reactions will not only turn out to be counter-productive, what we do usually increases the chance of the predicted problem happening! Taking an umbrella wouln't really increase the chance of a thunderstorm. But our negative forecasts actually work that way!

Examples of Predictions, Forecasts and other Supporting Beliefs

1. Not good enough (I am not safe)
Nobody will protect me
People are always having a go at me
It's going to happen again

2. Not good enough (I don't belong)
Nobody wants to know about me

3. Not good enough (I have no value, I am worthless,
Nobody values me
Nobody cares about me
People who say nice things to me don't mean them

4. Not good enough (I am powerless)
Other people manipulate me and control my life
I am trapped by others and cannot escape
All men/women are controllers

5. Not good enough (I am wrong, I am unsure)
It isn't fair
I won't get justice
I can't trust people
People don't trust me

6. Not good enough (My life is out of balance)
Other people have to fix my life for me
Who ever I am with is wrong.
Good times don't last
Nothing works any more

7. Not good enough (I don't exist, I am nothing)
People cannot see me

8. Not good enough (I am not real)
People will find out that I am a fake
People manipulate me
I will be rejected if they find out what I am really like

9. Not good enough (I am unlovable; unwanted)
Nobody loves me
Nobody wants me
People will ignore me

10. Not good enough (I am defective)
People can see I am in pain
People can see that I am defective
Someone else will heal, fix or repair me
Unless you heal me I will never get better
Nobody can heal my pain
People can tell there is something wrong with me

11. Not good enough (I have lost my spirit)
There is nothing to hope for
I must not get my hopes up

12. If it's happened to me three times before then it will happen again. There is nothing I can do to change that. *If it's rained every Thursday for the past three weeks then it will rain this Thursday.*

Other predictions and supporting beliefs:
The only solutions are outside of me
I cannot feel 'good enough' inside until I get other people to change the way they treat me

Activity Sheet CB-9

Keep this sheet private - Show it only to your therapist or counsellor or to close friends who will respect your confidentiality

Third Clue

Date __/__/__

My Forecasts, Expectations, Prophecies and Supporting Beliefs

Beliefs like these tell you there is a *direct connection* between your negative beliefs about yourself and what other people do to you (or what you think they will do) to trigger you. These beliefs help you forecast (make prophecies and predictions) to help you 'fit in' and to be less vulnerable, when you're with people who you expect to treat you in negative ways. The examples on the previous page will help you with these questions.

1. In what ways do you ***expect*** people will treat you or that you predict they will do to you that will hurt you the most? *Examples: 'I'll be ignored again'. They'll leave me out again. They'll criticise me again"*

   ____

   ____

2. What is it that you forecast other people <u>*won't do for you*</u> that you expect will hurt you the most? Example: *'People never listen to me'.*

   ____

3. How regularly do things like this happen to you? ____________________

4. Write down some of your familiar forecasts, you warn yourself could happen to you, things you need to watch out for, or expect other people will do to you. Write freely, using the first words that come into your mind. Here are just a few examples:

   OTHER PEOPLE ALWAYS ______________________________

   OTHER PEOPLE DON'T ______________________________

   NOBODY ______________________________

   EVERYBODY ______________________________

   I CAN'T TRUST OTHER PEOPLE TO ______________________________

   WHEN I ______________ OTHER PEOPLE USUALLY ______________________________

5. What do you sometimes tell yourself you need to do to protect yourself from these hurts? Example: *'I must not trust people'.* ______________________________

   ____

6. Do you get the feeling that your efforts to try to stop people doing these things, somehow increases the chances they then happen? ____________________

7. What is it that you most wanted to receive from other people at these times? What do you most want to receive today from other people, especially those you like or love? And that you usually don't receive.

   ____

   ____

8. When they give that magic something to you, do you sometimes reject it or feel uncomfortable accepting it? What do you do or say at the time, that limits your ability to truly receive it?

   ____

9. Recall two or more major events at times in your life when another person caused you feel either extreme emotional pain, terror or devastation. (It's safer not to identify them here. Use code names.)

   ____ | YOUR AGE THEN

   ____

Your Predicting and Your Forecasting patterns and your Self-fulfilling Prophecies are not 'invisible'

One of the other problems with having an unbalanced core belief is that while you may try to keep it hidden, some parts of it can be all too obvious to others.

Unknowingly, we send out very clear messages about our 'hidden' belief, so clear they might as well be flashing neon signs above our heads (and you or I ... the senders are the *only ones* who can't see it). Some of these messages are like advertisements in shop windows that invite people to 'apply within'. Some are like business cards, some work like messages in social network media or a profile on an internet dating site.

Is there a pattern?

Whatever your own 'message' might be, it will be reflected as similarities in the kind of people who seem attracted into your life. Do you notice the same or a similar pattern in the kinds of partners, friends, workmates, bosses, neighbours and even in your pets or your children?

Ask yourself if that could that have something to do with the wording of your 'advertisement'? For instance if your belief (as written on your flashing sign) is 'I get left out' that may be just the way most people will treat you.

It's not that they want to avoid you, it's more that they are going along with what you and your sign are projecting to them. However each time you get ignored or miss out on an invitation you'll become more convinced that it is 'them' who left you out, and the belief will seem more true. As a result, your sign may also grow a little larger!

When other people observe your belief flashing red light signal they can be attracted or repelled by it.

Person 'A' who holds a belief 'I am unlovable' will find ways to avoid getting close to self-confident people who might be ready to share a grown up loving relationship.

Taking an umbrella wouln't really increase the chance of a thunderstorm. But our negative forecasts actually work that way!

What happens when you unconsciously advertise your negative core belief for everyone to see)

At the same time he or she will send out flashing red light signals that ***increase the chance those same grown up love sharing people will avoid him.***

And at the same time his signals will ***attract unwelcome attention from others who hold equally low beliefs about themselves*** and who recognise 'A' as someone who is unlikely to reject them.

Look at the following imaginary 'core belief advertisements'. Because other people can read them clearly what kind of person might be attracted by signs that say:

I would love to help you with your problems. No fees no conditions.

I will do anything I can to stop you feeling your pain. Open 24 hours a day.

I can help you feel more valuable and improve your self esteem. Just walk all over me.

Just tell me what I have to do for you and I'll do it. No appointment needed,

Your self-fulfilling prophecy

This is how, quite unconsciously, you often attract into your life (and your relationships) the kind of people who match up with your core belief. You notice you feel comfortable having them around you. You may not be as relaxed with someone whose core belief doesn't fit in with yours.

Whatever that kind of person then does to you seems to confirm that your belief is still as true today as it has been in the past.

What you advertised for is what you got, and what you expected is what happened, a perfect example of a self-fulfilling prophecy. Except that it doesn't need to be this way! Once you balance your two opposite beliefs the problems you forecast don't happen.

Activity Sheet CB-10

Keep this sheet private - Show it only to your therapist or counsellor or to close friends who will respect your confidentiality

Date _ _/ _ _/ _ _

Third Clue

What messages do your 'hidden' beliefs send out to the world?

Don't take it too seriously, but what do you think your own flashing sign or your 'apply within' advertisement might be saying to other people? Whatever your own 'message' might be, if it exists it will be reflected as similarities in the kind of people who seem attracted into your life. If you notice the same or a similar pattern in partners, friends, workmates, bosses, neighbours and even in your pets or your children, could it just be something to do with the wording of your 'advertisement'. In the boxes below, write some possible messages, signs or advertisements that could reflect the kind of people, events or things that you repeatedly seem to attract into your life. Do keep this exercise light hearted though, as in examples below.

EXAMPLES:

Need something to lean on - use my shoulder. If you can't call in, just phone and I'll come to you

Specialist helping others with their emotional trauma and excess guilt - please deposit your problems here - open 24 hours

Weak passive person seeks partner to walk all over them. No special shoes required

Bored with life? - free seats available - let me entertain you now

Are you inconsiderate? Walk in now - no need to knock - special welcome for selfish users

Need to be admired or adored - apply within for full service - no charge, I'll pay you

Worried? Insecure? Let's get together (Is this notice OK?)

Garage sale - my time going cheap today

Doormat available - one size fits all users

Please treat me the way you'd like to treat me - you know best

Guaranteed unlimited compassion for your pain - free two year trial - your time refunded in full if not satisfied

Position vacant. Critical person needed to help me understand why it's always my fault.

I'm only as good as you make me feel - awaiting your instructions

Give me your sick, your tired, your useless, your bored - My refugee rescue service is open seven days a week

I need a bigger burden - let me carry yours too

Wanted people who will ignore me - (don't bother to let me know, just turn up and ignore me when you are ready)

Free party hire - everything you need for a good time (Your application has already been approved.)

My body is an amusement park - not a temple - Trespassers Will Not be Prosecuted

Need someone to stand up for *your rights*? - My free life support system is yours for the asking

No user serviceable parts inside

Clue Number Four
Your Skills and Abilities create wonderful gifts
(for other people)

Most people discover, sooner or later that they have developed a few very powerful skills that, when they are working at their usual occupation, help them cope better with their old unbalanced beliefs These are described as *compensating skills* because these special talents or abilities seem to help 'balance the books', in that the gifts they help create *for other people* seem to offset the bad thoughts or feelings that go with our unbalanced negative beliefs about "not being good enough."

Giving your particular kind of special gift seems as if it should compensate for whatever particular kind of negative energy is associated with your individual belief.

Your special skills are almost always reflected in the work you do, or your professional skill area. They are usually the key to your chosen career and your success in the impersonal working world.

I am always wrong becomes a successful lawyer

A person who has an unbalanced core belief *'I am always wrong'* might compensate for this belief by developing powerful skills that help them argue (successfully) their they and their beliefs are *not wrong.*

This attracts that person towards situations during their secondary schooling where they gain prestige by debating and winning arguments about 'right' and 'wrong'. They go on to study law and become a successful lawyer, a judge (or perhaps a politician) thanks to their compensating skills and the gift those skills help them create for other people whether they defend an individual or a whole group who are being treated unfairly as if they were 'wrong'.

Compensating Skill based Gifts - My own example: My career over 64 years has always been focused on helping other people value themselves. I did this in the past to try to get them *to see me* as more valuable than I felt inside or *at least to get them to tell me* I was more valuable in their eyes. My old core belief was "I have no value".

Gift: *Helping others feel more valuable*

Gift: *Showing others new ways they can become more valuable*

WARNING! Don't try this at home

Your powerful Compensating skills and gifts that suceed at work have the opposite effect when you try to use them in your personal life. Often they create major relationship problems.

Fourth Clue
Your Compensating skills and the gifts they create for other people.

Aim: To identify your professional or work-related skills that you've developed so far in life and which for many years helped to hide or offset your negative core belief. Try to understand that these are real gifts, gifts that you'll get to keep after you've balanced your old Core Belief. They are also a significant pointer to help you identify your old core belief because the kinds of gifts you give other people are usually the mirror opposite of your own Core Belief.

People often experience difficulties with Activity sheets CB-11 and CB-12. Their negative core belief tells them they shouldn't say positive things about themselves or recognise their true skills and gifts even in an activity sheet! (see Clue number 6)

Allow yourself the freedom, just this once, to recognise your special skills and remind yourself that after you have balanced a Core Belief not only will you retain these skills but they will work better for you than ever before.

Compensating skills create gifts for others

He or she will become highly regarded for their ability to help others who have to battle political or legal issues about being right or wrong.

However that does not mean that the person is now free of their original belief. Underneath they are still convinced they remain 'wrong' much of the time.

Their compensating skill-based gifts may hide the old belief from the world, but they don't make it go away.

Each time they <u>fail</u> in an attempt to help others to be "not wrong" *they will connect straight back to their original pain about being wrong.*

I can't fix anything becomes an IT expert

Imagine a negative belief *'Nothing works for me'* that originally helped the child 'make sense of' their family life, which they couldn't fix, because it was unfixable.

> ***Can you sense the paradox of a protection system that is trying to get someone else to help ease your hurting at the same time as it is trying to hide that pain from them!***
>
> *Nikki Nemerouf*

That's what led them in their teens to develop a whole set of problem solving and *'making things work'* skills that compensated for their old belief. Those incredible skills opened up careers in Information Technology and similar advanced complex problem solving professions. It could just as easily have led to a career in counselling or even medicine.

Their problem solving and fixing skills compensated for the old belief, and helped keep it hidden from other people. It also helped hide it from the person with that belief.

A belief *'I don't know how'* could encourage the development in grown up life of a highly skilled analytical and enquiring mind as compensation. The result could be a career as a research scientist, an engineer or business analyst.

A belief that *'I am confused'* might well be offset by compensating skills that help that person become very well organised and this can lead on to careers in teaching (mathematics or science) psychology or editing.

So these skills help you create and share wonderful gifts for other people, but the's a "catch". This kind of gift comes with a price tag attached.

Compensating gifts help you hide your negative beliefs from you too

However giving these gifts is not only meant to hide your Core Belief from others. Most compensating gifts also help hide a Core Belief from you as well.

- ***I am very good at understanding people.*** *(Is this how I try to cope with a prediction that no one really understands me?)*
- ***I help others solve their problems.*** *(Perhaps this helps me with my fear that I can't solve my own problems)*
- ***I help others feel trustworthy.*** *(Does this help me cope with my own thoughts or feelings that I am not reliable or trustworthy?)*

These free gifts comes with a price tag attached

You and I use our Compensating Skills to create real gifts for other people. However if we over-do the giving it may no longer feel like a gift. For example, if I feel I am un-lovable then I can make too much drama about my giving my love to other people. I may think it's hidden but somewhere inside in return for my gifts there is an all too obvious catch. Perhaps in retrurn I expect the receiver to *see me* as more lovable or *hope they'll tell me* I am more lovable even though I don't feel that way inside.

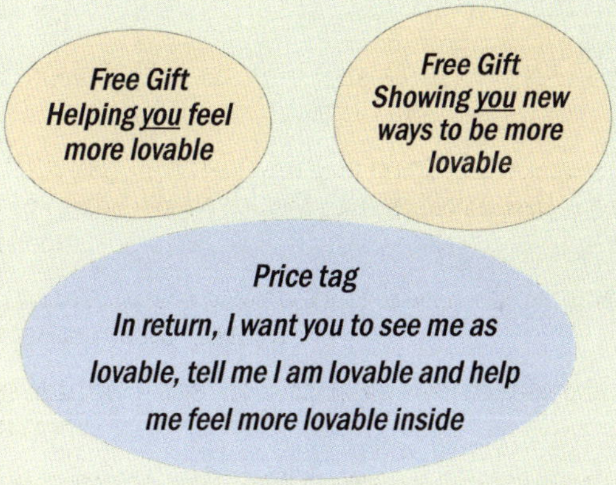

The trouble is that your price tag (the reward you expect in return for your gift) is too obvious. People may accept your gift but they will automatically resist giving you what you want in return. They can feel inside that your gift was not given freely. It was not a real gift at all and you are seen as not being authentic. Result. Your old belief will win again!

- *I help others to feel safer. (Am I doing this so they will help me feel safer too?)*
- ***I help fix things for other people.*** *(Is this because deep down I feel I am no good at fixing things about my own life?)*

Although these gifts work so well in impersonal working environments the same person is unlikely to have much success using the same skills in their own personal relationship issues.

Don't try to use them at home

The same gifts don't work as well when you try to share them in your personal life. Often the same skills that are so successful at work set up major relationship problems at home.

They only work in impersonal situations

Compensating skills work best in *impersonal* situations such as in the person's professional or working environment.

In their private life where people need to use much more *personal* communication the same skills no longer work. You may find yourself constantly being disempowered at home where your professional skills and gifts are not acknowledged and there's no impartial work related clientele to back them up. So your old core belief wins again.

The older you get the less they work

Another problem is that although compensating skills work quite well for a start and the gifts to others are at first greatly appreciated, sooner or later they start to lose their power to hide the old belief. That's usually got something to do with the the hidden price tags attached to the gifts.

Compensating skills and gifts can become authentic

They may have started out as useful ways of hiding a Core Belief from others and from you as well.

However, once you have balanced your negative and positive beliefs your skills and gifts remain but they are enhanced. You don't lose them.

Instead, after balancing, they become real gifts, helping you to help others in functional ways.

As you get to know and appreciate your own collection of special skills you find them becoming part of your authentic personality.

In the future, the more your old core belief is balanced, these same skills will start to reflect the 'real' you in positive ways.

You can learn which special personal skills you use, the gifts you give and see how they help you compensate for your unbalanced beliefs, using Activity sheets CB-11 and CB-12.

The 'bank overdraft' effect

Giving gifts to other people is supposed to help reduce your feelings of not being good enough. But even when your compensating skills are working well, you somehow still don't seem to wind up with the good feelings you expected when you give your gifts away.

Unbalanced core beliefs work a bit like having a big overdraft loan at the bank. No matter what you do that is good or positive seems to get drained away soon afterwards.

It's as if the good feelings you hoped to feel from giving people gifts all get used up just like a new deposit all gets used up paying interest on the debt while the big overdraft remains the same.

In this case the negative power of your old unbalanced belief remains unchanged even when you have a big win.

My own examples:

My career over the past years had always been focused on helping other people value themselves, my gift to them.

I did this back then to try to get them *to see me* as more valuable than I felt inside or *at least to get them to tell me* I was more valuable in their eyes. It never worked. My old core belief "I have no value" stayed firmly in place.

Today I still do the same things, use the same skills, give the same gifts but now I seek nothing in return. Surprise!

People value me far more often because I am not applying any pressure. If someone occasionally doesn't value me I don't worry. It doesn't matter. Best of all, I don't get triggered the way I used to back then because no matter how hard i tried they didn't value me.

You can learn which special personal skills you use, the gifts you give and see how they help you compensate for your unbalanced beliefs, using Activity sheets CB-11 and CB-12.

Your old, unbalanced core beliefs tell you that who you are and how much you matter in the World is determined by other people, not by you. This is untrue.

After you have identified and balanced your core beliefs you can expect more joy because there is no 'overdraft' eating away at your positive feelings.

Your same compensating skills are still there, but now they will work to create positive gifts since there is no need any longer for them to waste your energy offsetting your negative beliefs.

IMPORTANT - What gifts do other people 'take home' after they have been working with you?

If your core belief is telling you that you are not good enough, it's understandable you'll find it specially difficult completing Activity sheets CB-11 and CB-12 on the next two pages, asking you to describe things you do really well in your work or profession.

But these sheets are *<u>not</u> asking you to describe you, or the good things <u>you do</u> at work.* They are asking about what you give to others at work, things they feel ***are good for them.***

Stick with it. This is a very important clue. Focus on the gifts other people 'take home' after working with you.

My second old core belief was about my not being able to make things work "I am a klutz"

You may not be too surprised to learn that another of my useful compensating skills is my ability to help other people *make things work*.

One of my most vulnerable inner selves associated with this is my poor inner klutz, illustrated here.

These days after balancing the two opposite beliefs I still sometimes can't get something to work.

The difference is that while I may still be bothered by this I no longer get triggered or have an F reaction about it.

That gives me more time and energy to do whatever I need to do to focus on the problem calmly and quietly and get it fixed.

Activity Sheet CB- 11

Keep this sheet private - Show it only to your therapist or counsellor or to close friends who will respect your confidentiality

Fourth Clue - Part A

Date __/__/__

My skills and gifts that offset my unbalanced old core beliefs

Until you start balancing your core beliefs, your most common way of offsetting the imbalance is to rely on your special skills to help other people. Example: *I help others solve their problems (Am I hoping they will help me fix mine in return?) I act strong and confident (Is this how I help hide my own weakness from others) I help others feel trusted or safe (Will this help them to trust me?) I am very good at understanding people (Will this help me understand myself better?)* **Acknowledging the way you give gifts like these to offset your old hidden core belief helps you get closer to discovering what that belief might be.**

1. Think of whatever you give others as something they "take home" after you have helped them. Your compensating skills helped you to create those special gifts. When other people tell you how much they appreciate your special skills, abilities how would ***they*** (not you) describe what it is they have gained personally from working with you?

The gifts you give to others using your special skills as you describe them here, are a mirror, a clue that points towards the belief you are trying hardest to hide or overcome within you by giving these gifts.

2. What are your special skills or abilities that help you create those gifts for other people? What do you do that is special in the way you use your abilities to help others cope with their problems?

3. When you achieve success using these special skills, how long and how strongly do you continue to feel a sense of joy or accomplishment?

4. How do you feel if people reject your offer to help them the way you want to, using your special skills,

5. Remember a time when you used your special skills to help someone but that person then criticised your efforts, They failed to appreciate your help (or you discovered your gifts were of no help to them). How did you react? Pain, anger, loss guilt or shame? For how long did those negative feelings continue ? How bad were they?

6. If you were unable to share your special skills or gifts with people any more, how would you feel about yourself?

7. When you share your special skills and abilities as gifts to others, what might it be ***inside you*** that you could be trying to hide from them?

8. Which of your special gifts, skills or abilities do you try to use to improve your personal relationships? How succesful are they when you use them in personal situations, away from work?

Activity Sheet CB- 12

Keep this sheet private - Show it only to your therapist or counsellor or to close friends who will respect your confidentiality

Fourth Clue - Part B

Date __/__/__

My skills and gifts that offset my unbalanced old core beliefs

Until you start balancing your core beliefs, your most common way of offsetting the imbalance is to rely on your special skills to compensate for, or hide the core pain you feel when a Core Belief is triggered. **Acknowledging the way you use these skills to offset a belief helps you get closer to discovering what the belief is.** The exercise below is one that worries some people. Try to accept that it is only an imaginary event. The point is to get you thinking about (when you are no longer around) which of your professional or work related skills are most likely to be remembered by work colleagues or clients as real gifts . Those are your compensating skills.

1. Imagine that you met with a sudden and unfortunate accident and will be absent from your workplace for several years. In fact you may never get back to that job again. A few weeks after your departure, some of your work and business associates are gathered together and they start remembering all the good the things you have done for people as part of your work.

Some of your business colleagues, your customers, students, or clients each say a few words about the things you did for them during your working life. They describe what you gave them as gifts

They might say, sadly, how much they miss not having you around to do those things for them any longer. They may talk about how you used your special skills when you worked here and how much they appreciated them, but their main emphasis will be not about who you are or how you did things, more about what they gained from you.

Hint: These people are not your close friends. Some barely know you. They will not be describing personal qualities like friendship or kindness, honesty or good communication skills. They will be describing what they felt that ***you did for them*** as part of your work or in your profession. How would they describe some of the gifts you gave them, when you were using your compensating skills.

____

____

2. Imagine a small group of four or five people from your work environment, your colleagues, your clients, those who work under you; people who supervise or lead you, your students or people who you train. They are all talking about working with you *in a positive way* when a stranger joins the group and asks each person ....

*"So, what is the **most valuable gift** you gain from working with ----- (your first name) ------?*

What might each person then say about your gift to them as they see it? (You might include people here from your previous work environments as well as your present work associates)

PERSON A: ______________________________

PERSON B: ______________________________

PERSON C: ______________________________

PERSON D: ______________________________

3. Think back to a time when you gave freely and unconditionally of yourself to another person or a project in your working or professional environment and you received some wonderful appreciation or compliments. Your gift to them worked! What were you doing? How did you come to be there? How did you feel while you were giving so much of yourself? How did you feel at that time, when you and your gift to them were truly appreciated?

____

____

A Quick way to reduce the power of an old Core Belief

History has taught us that *not talking* about any kind of problem helps that problem grow stronger. On the other hand, talking about a problem usually reduces the power of that problem.

The more a problem increases our vulnerability, the more important it is to bring it out into the open, to talk about it. But too often those high vulnerability issues are the same ones that don't get brought up and aren't talked about.

An old negative core belief is a good example.

As you read on you'll discover just how holding on to one old core belief can create the some of the worst problems in your life.

But those old beliefs are also closely related to your deepest vulnerability. So they remain hidden, not talked about and that means they grow and grow.

The good news. Once you name your old core belief and balance it, it begins to lose its power.

The more you talk about it openly the weaker it becomes.

At the heart of every core belief sits an underlying belief *"Who I am and how much I matter in the World is decided not by me but by people around me."* <u>This is not true</u> and as soon as you start questioning this you start escaping from your old core beliefs. Notice how closely this next clue, your Predictions and Expectations are connected to thoughts about how your underlying sense of "...who I am" is undermined by thinking too much about "...what I expect they are going to do to me".

Fifth Clue - Your Family History

<u>Aim:</u> Looking back at your childhood can be one of the most significant clues in identifying your own core issue and an old negative core belief. However, working back through your family history is individual and personal.

The case study at the end of this section will give you an idea of just how significant family history can be in terms of identifying where a Core Belief came from and how it helped a person to "fit in" or "make sense of" their life as a child.

You will have an opportunity to work on your family history when you complete activity sheet CB-13 and CB-15 where you'll be looking it the first of the five gifts that your old core belief gave you.

A belief that is about anyone or anything outside of you is <u>not a core belief</u>.

A belief that involves a specific action or specific doing word <u>is not a core belief.</u>

If there is even a suggestion that you might be better off obeying an old 'how not to live rule' <u>it is not a core belief.</u> Core beliefs do not offer choices or options.

If you can reverse, get rid of, erase or remove a negative belief this confirms that it was <u>not a core belief.</u>

Clue number Five
Your Childhood and your Family History

At this stage you will have already looked at four different clues that may, by now, be giving you ideas about your own unbalanced old negative core belief.

Looking back at your childhood and your family history can provide one more very important clue, particularly when you remember that your core beliefs were created to help you fit in with or make sense of whatever was happening to you as a child.

Think back about your childhood and perhaps some of the situations where you, as a small child may have had to make sense of things that you should not have been experiencing and should not have had to make sense of, your ACEs (Adverse Childhood Experiences).

Please take it slowly, because remembering your childhood may be difficult, or even painful for you and is it is important that you protect yourself if you start to find yourself becoming too emotional as you work through this step.

For example you might remember situations where you experienced neglect, injustice, dishonest parenting, parents with addictions, trauma, violence, abuse, excessive control or just feelings of vulnerability, fear or shame.

Whatever you experienced, particularly if it happened regularly it's quite likely that you as a small child felt a need for:

1. A "because" that helped you make sense of and accept what was happening to you *(even though it should not have been happening).*

or

2. A "because" that just helped you "fit in" better in your family or at school.

or both.

In many cases the only "because" that seemed to work (at that time) may have been backed up by the understandable belief held by most small children about the adults and elder siblings in the family.

"*.. it cannot be their fault. So it must be my fault."*

This in turn is exactly what leads to the creation of a child's core belief:

"I am not good enough because I .....

"I can't because I don't know how .....

"I am not good enough because I am doing something the wrong way .... "

"I am a failure because ...."

"I am unlovable or shameful because ...."

"I don't deserve to be happy because ...."

If believing any one of these thoughts increased your sense of "fitting in" a little better or helped you "make sense" of daily life as you knew it, then (untrue though it was) this "because belief" would appear to be working for you,, so every day the belief would begin to seem a little more true and grow a bit stronger.

Was there a little chair you had to sit in with labels on it and rules about what you could not do?

Some people recall a childhood feeling as if there was a little chair with labels on it that described who they were supposed to be in their family. It wasn't comfortable but the only way to fit in with the rest of the family was sit in that little chair and wear its labels and follow the rules about what you were not allowed to do or say or not even to feel or think!

In an extreme example imagine a family including Mum, Dad and three older siblings who were all a bit

My experimental ACE survey is available free as a pdf file, sent by e-mail
Just e-mail me
bligh4@growingaware.com
... and I'll send you my latest ACE survey so you can calculate your own ACE score.
(It's free of course)
Or download it from my website
www.ACE.realme1.com

emotionally unbalanced. You come into that family and though only a tiny child you happened to have perfect emotional balance. You were not going to fit in. That was until you started believing *"I'm unbalanced"* It wasn't true, but that didn't matter because now you felt at least you had a place in your family and you could 'fit in'.

You sat in your chair feeling unbalanced but suddenly that felt much better than not fitting in!

Common little chair labels:

I am stupid
I am slow
I am wrong

At the time it was a necessity, which is why we acknowledge that the old core belief back then was giving you a useful "gift" and how it helped you *back then.*

It's important to recognise what happened back then as the first 'gift' to you from your old belief. While it may seem strange to refer to this creation of the child's unbalanced core belief as a "gift" for the child, at that time it was a necessity.

You could describe this as a *'because' you needed as a child when you shouldn't have needed a 'because'.*

The more the belief seems to 'make sense' or helped you 'fit in' better, the more it would seem in a small child's mind as though it "must be true" and so it becomes more firmly embedded.

In a way it's a bit like a jigsaw puzzle where you suddenly find one piece that seems to fit perfectly and once it's in place all the other parts of the jigsaw puzzle seem to come together. Except in this case the bit that seemed to fit actually didn't belong there at all. It only seemed to fit at the time.

In a functional ACE free family environment a child would not have needed to take on such negative beliefs.

You'll have an opportunity to work a bit more on your family history when you complete activity sheets CB - 13 and CB-15 where you will be looking it all five of the gifts that your old core belief gave you back then and realise why they are still real gifts today.

What could be a very good idea at this stage would be to look at some of the case studies in this book and in book CBal-2 because in every case study you'll find that there are references to the individual's family history and in each case these are important clues that help you identify that person's old unbalanced or negative core belief.

What were some of the special 'family' rules you had to follow to be allowed to fit in?

The second thing to look at in your childhood are your old family rules. Some may have been unspoken and yet those rules will have seemed very real and very powerful to you. Typical rule *"You must not cause your Mother ./ Father to feel hurt or pain."*

The penalties for not sticking to those family rules could have been physical but more often they were emotional which means they hurt a small child far more deeply and stayed as powerful forces in your life far longer than physical pain. Example:

You must not talk about_ _ *any thing that's not allowed* _ _

Penalties:

Withdrawing of love or affection
Shaming Ridicule
Ignoring, rejecting or abandoning you

In adult life, the outcome, because of the way you were punished emotionally for breaking rules, is described as an *"unhealed emotional wound"*. It's still there and it's closely connected to your core belief.

Often there were even similar penalties for daring to question unspoken rules. *"Not only were they not discussable but you could not even talk about why they were undiscussable"* (Pia Mellody)

Appreciation

Appreciate the way the old core beliefs helped you as a child and why you must never try to "get rid of them."

Why did they come into your life? Strange as it may seem, as soon as you begin nolw to appreciate *the way they helped you as a child* they begin to lose some of their intensity.

Why it's so important.

At this stage you may be wondering why this understanding and appreciation about how your the old belief helped you back then is so important? Actually it's essential.

During this program you are discovering the reasons why you can't balance a negative core belief *until* you understand its history and accept and understand why it initially came into your life *to help you.*

Activity Sheet CB-13

Keep this sheet private - Show it only to your therapist or counsellor or to close friends who will respect your confidentiality

Fifth Clue - Your Family History
Fitting in

Date __/__/__

Can you recall a childhood feeling as if there was a little chair with labels on it that described *who you were supposed to be* in your family.

The little chair wasn't at all comfortable but the only way you were allowed to be at the family table was if you sat in your little chair and became the person that fitted the labels.

Imagine what those labels might have said ..... things about who you were supposed to be or why you had to follow the rules about what you were .... Rules about what you were not not allowed to do or say or not even to feel or think!

1. What might have been some of the labels on your little chair that you had to sit in?

Labels about who you were: ______________________________

____

2. What were some of the special 'family' rules you had to follow to be allowed to fit in? Some may have been unspoken and yet they seemed very real to you.

Family Rules about what you were NOT allowed to do: ____________________

____

Family Rules about what you were NOT allowed to say: ____________________

____

Family Rules about what you were NOT allowed to feel: ____________________

____

Family Rules about what you were NOT allowed to think: ____________________

____

Anything else you remember having to do or having to be, to help you fit in:

____

Sixth Clue
Uncomfortable with praise, compliments, success

This happens so often that one of the ways to identify a core belief is just to ask yourself what kind of compliment (about you) can make you feel most uncomfortable. Do you find it difficult to accept success? There's your sixth clue.

While you have powerful unbalanced negative beliefs in place, your sense of reality may be so tied up, polarised, bound and distorted that you may not want to see the positive parts within you. Until you begin your balancing process, you may reject, even fight the reality if someone tries to tell you that you have a positive side.

On the other hand you'll find it easier to collect 'evidence' that seems to prove that your negative core beliefs are true and harder to see evidence to the contrary!

Read *"The Case of the Stolen selfEsteem"* a fictional story about a core detective battling false negative evidence in book CBal-2. It has a happy ending.

Why is this so? Because part of the way old core beliefs operate is to use the same *fixed, repeated, automatic patterns you learned in childhood* to keep you from feeling the pain of being re-connected to those childhood memories.

Unfortunately, accepting a sincere compliment would connect you to that old belief so the same automatic pattern comes in to block positive messages while accepting negative ones.

A bit too ready to take on an insult or rejection?

Are you sometimes a bit too ready to take on an insult or rejection? If one of your beliefs is *'I am not worth listening to'* you'll notice *every instance* where people ignore your advice (and you'll be hurt by that). You may totally miss a situation where someone compliments you on a worthwhile suggestion. Or you may hear the words but get no joy from the compliment (you may even devalue it) wondering to yourself. *'Why is he pretending? What's he trying to get from me?'*

You will miss the truth because you are so busy trying to cope with the false belief. The problem you so wished you could get rid of is actually being helped to stay put.

Activity Sheet CB-14

Keep this sheet private - Show it only to your therapist or counsellor or to close friends who will respect your confidentiality

Date _ _/ _ _/ _ _

Sixth Clue - Uncomfortable accepting Success. Rejecting praise for something you did well or a positive observation about who you are

Work fast. Do not spend a lot of time on any one reaction. Only score the ones you do more often. If you feel your score on any line is between 1 to 4 then score a zero. But, if you feel your score is on the red 5 to 10 side just pick one number somewhere between 5 and 10 that you think or feel might indicate how each statement applies to you at present. Accurate scoring is not necessary. Wondering whether 6 or 7? - 8 or 9? Either one will give the same results.

How comfortable do you feel accepting praise or appreciation? How long do the good feelings last?

*Very comfortable 0_ 1_ 2_ 3_ 4 _**5_ 6_7_ 8_ 9_10** Good feelings only last for _ _ _ _ (short time) _ _*

How comfortable are you about accepting success? How long do the good feelings last?

*Very comfortable 0_ 1_ 2_ 3_ 4 _**5_ 6_7_ 8_ 9_10** Good feelings only last for _ _ _ _ _ (short time) _ _*

When you do achieve success, is it only temporary? Do you lose it again ?

*I hang on to it 0_ 1_ 2_ 3_ 4 _**5_ 6_7_ 8_ 9_10** It doesn't last*

Do you sometimes avoid an opportunity to be more successful?

*I Never avoid another chance 0_ 1_ 2_ 3_ 4 _**5_ 6_7_ 8_ 9_10** I Always avoid another chance*

When you really do deserve praise how do you react?

*Delighted, Good feelings last for _ _ _ (time) _ _ 0_ 1_ 2_ 3_ 4 _**5_ 6_7_ 8_ 9_10** Very uncomfortable*

Do you find it easier to accept 'evidence' that seems to prove that your not good enough feelings are real and harder to see evidence to the contrary?

*I don't do this 0_ 1_ 2_ 3_ 4 _**5_ 6_7_ 8_ 9_10** I do this all the time*

Are you sometimes a bit too ready to take on an insult or rejection?

*Never 0_ 1_ 2_ 3_ 4 _**5_ 6_7_ 8_ 9_10** I so often feel insulted or rejected*

My total for all the questions above _ _ _ _

The higher your score the more your old core belief is getting in the way, stopping you accepting praise or appreciation that you deserve.

Expect your score to get lower, after you balance your old core belief with a positive belief.

Your Seventh clue

Five 'gifts' from your old negative core beliefs

Recognising, honouring the five gifts and accepting them as real gifts, then understanding how and why you received them, is more than just another clue. It's a very important step in balancing your old negative beliefs with your positive ones.

There are five gifts that you discover along with your acceptance of your own particular old or negative core belief. When we are trying to understand our old core beliefs we need to acknowledge that they have, in the past, served an essential purpose. Back then they were not 'bad' or 'wrong' just very down-to-earth and very practical ways of helping us, making us believe that we had no ability to change things about us we would have liked to change. They told us it was 'little me who *had to change our belief system* to survive.

In my case, a negative belief that *'I have no value as a child'* helped me to adapt, to grow up and become a 'little adult' very rapidly. This was what my parents demanded of me before I was accepted as a fitting member of the family and it was my negative belief that helped me to complete my adaption. I had actually become a 'small but very responsible hard working adult' by around nine years of age.

Your first gift - you 'made it' through childhood!

The fact that you 'made it' and were able to fit in with your family is itself the primary gift from our core belief. Developing a Core Belief was essential in order for you either to "fit in" better or "make sense of" what was happening in your family or both. (even though that belief was not true).

Recognising these as real 'gifts' is an essential step towards balancing your old unbalanced beliefs with positive ones.

Seventh Clue - Your Five Core Gifts

Aim: One of the reasons core belief balancing succeeds so well is that instead of blaming or punishing the old core belief you acknowledge that it had a very important part to play in your childhood and your teen years.

Remind yourself that the gifts that it gave you then were all that stood between you and an intolerable level of pain and vulnerability. The old belief helped you survive, helped you fit in, helped you make sense of things that you should not have needed to make sense of it all and it kept you always hoping that if you did that, things would get better

This understanding helps you to realise that core belief balancing is a positive process. In particular, notice the last gift, the gift of Balance.

This is why, when you are preparing for balancing your old and your new beliefs that you first reassure the old belief that you appreciate what it did for you at that time and that you unserstand why this was necessary at that time.

The second gift - your compensating skills and the gifts they create for other people are the key to your success in the world.

The second gift, strange as it may seem, is that it was your own negative core belief helped you develop your "Compensating Skills" as an adaption which you, as you grew up discovered helped make up for what your negative beliefs told you about yourself

You also discovered your powerful compensating skills helped you hide the old belief from yourselves and other people by giving them your special gifts.

You might like to go back to page 49 to read more about compensating skills and problems of giving a 'gift with the hidden price tag'.

This usually works quite well for a start and is often the key to your chosen career and your success in the world around you.

If you hadn't had that particular negative core belief you would either not have developed those particular skills at all or not developed them as well as you have.

You can honour the way you use those particular skills to create gifts for other people and how that has proved a tremendous benefit to you, particularly in your professional life or career. But in the end if all that achieves is to compensate for your old negative core belief you won't realise its full worth. However, you will though, once you balance your positive and negative beliefs. What you'll find is that the skills and gifts are actually enhanced, because they are now true and genuine with no hidden price tag.

The difference is that you will no longer be using your skills and gifts just to offset the unbalanced negative energy. They are still a tremendous gift for you and it was your old negative core belief that caused you to develop them.

Your third gift - The personal power that comes with acknowledging your vulnerability and your imperfections. No need to hide them, no need to get triggered when things go wrong.

Sometimes I really am not good enough. Sometimes I make mistakes, Sometimes I am not lovable. But that's normal - No need to get triggered any more

Grown up humility

This third gift is very special. Without it you could not become an authentic mature grown-up. It's sometimes described as 'grown-up or adult humility' or in simple terms your ability to accept that as a grown-up you will always be a bit vulnerable, to accept your real faults, real failings, real foul-ups, to acknowledge that you are wrong sometimes and that you do make mistakes. Acceopt that you will always have a negative side to you, but the reality is that you can balance it with your positive side.

Your old core belief helped you to do these things but until now you may have been doing them in negative ways. *Surprise, after balancing your two beliefs these same patterns become positive skills!*

> The first four are gifts that the negative core belief has given you in the past. The fifth and the most important gift is the gift that it is going to continue to give you in the future.

It takes courage to openly acknowledge your vulnerability in a grown up way. Accepting this feeling inside you at first is still a bit scary. But it has an upside.

Acknowledging your vulnerability increases your personal power

Grown-up humility is a quiet, yet positive acceptance of reality. It differs from 'ordinary' humility in that it is a mark of your inner strength, it's not negative and it is low in intensity.

It's a sign of strength, of your personal power and a confirmation that you are becoming an authentic grown-up.

Grown up humility gives us the ability to recognize how sometimes or on certain occasions you and I simply are just "not good enough" and that's okay. Once your core beliefs have been balanced this becomes a healthy aspect of being human and nothing to worry about. No need to get triggered.

Your fourth gift - empathy *"I know how other people feel" "I can support them when they make mistakes" "I can reassure them when they are troubled by their own old core beliefs."* Plus your ability *(only if you choose)* to fit in with difficult situations and with difficult people

The fourth gift that your old negative core beliefs give you is the skill of empathy which helps you connect with other people who share similar negative core beliefs or who make the same kind of mistakes you make.

You have not forgotten your childhood "fitting in" skills that came with your old core belief.

This gift also helps you 'fit in' with difficult people or cope with difficult situations just as it helped you do that in your childhood. But, in future you can choose to do this, only when and if and how much, no longer because you give in to pressure or feel you 'have to'.

The final and most important gift - the future gift - The gift of Balance

The final gift is the gift of balance, the ability and the power that comes when you can sit between your negative belief and your positive belief and recognise how wonderful it is to have that sense of balance. This is a gift that you continue to receive every day of your life from now on.

If you didn't still have your old unbalanced core belief you couldn't do your balancing. It still has a place and will always have a place in your life.. Instead, you maintain your negative belief but in a totally different role as a functional counterbalance to the positive one.

Weakening the old belief *by itself* would have left you feeling *too positive* and in the end just as unbalanced, except that the imbalance would now be in the opposite direction.

With no negative belief you might, for example, find it hard to recognise that you sometimes still wind up doing things in a negative way. We need to keep that part.

Understanding the gifts may help explain why we all need to balance our old negative beliefs with positive ones, rather than just try throw the negative ones out. To lose the old belief would leave us feeling *too positive* and in the end just as unbalanced, only in the opposite direction. With no negative belief we would find it hard to recognise that we sometimes do make mistakes, to acknowledge this openly and do something practical about fixing them.

Once you stop being driven by the painful side of your core beliefs you begin to experience the positive nature of your real and natural self in relation to that same issue. This awareness of your natural self, and your sense of being who you really are, forms a part of your healthy reality.

Experiencing and sharing your inner gifts increases the number of positive ways that people can now find to communicate with you and respond to your best features, something your negative beliefs always seemed to stop happening.

Appreciation

Appreciate the way the old core beliefs helped you as a child and why you must never try to "get rid of them."

Why did they come into your life? Strange as it may seem, as soon as you begin nolw to appreciate *the way they helped you as a child* they begin to lose some of their intensity.

Why it's so important.

At this stage you may be wondering why this understanding and appreciation about how your the old belief helped you back then is so important? Actually it's essential.

During this program you are discovering the reasons why you can't balance a negative core belief *until* you understand its history and accept and understand why it initially came into your life *to help you*.

Why the gift of balance is so important

Let's take my own negative core belief that *"I am not good enough because I have no value"*. I balanced it with a belief in my own value, in a rather special way.

Back and the bad old days I was always giving things away to people, in the futile hope that it might encourage them to value me. Because of my negative core belief of course it never worked. But I had a feeling deep inside that even after I had done my balancing I still would like to be able to give things away to people (sometimes). Today, I say to myself *"The more I give my gifts to others, the more valuable I really am"*. That's the gift of balance

Let's suppose for example that my positive belief had became over-developed and my old core belief self became too weak. That would mean I would be out of balance and going around making a fuss about how wonderful I was giving my gifts away. Before long I would be a pain in the butt for people around me (and they would then stop valuing me).

Maintaining and embracing my old negative core belief allows me to maintain a nice flexible balance between my grown up humility and my sense of having true value. It doesn't matter any longer whether or not other people recognize it.

That's my fifth gift and I couldn't have that gift if I didn't continue to use and embrace my old negative core belief to help me maintain a proper balance with my positive one.

That's why I continue to emphasise how important it is that you are careful not to put yourself in the hands of a counsellor or psychotherapist who suggests they can help you "remove", or "get rid of" your negative core belief.

Not only will they fail but they can do real damage while they are trying.

Recognising these "gifts" is one of the points emphasised by Nikki Nemerouf in his teaching about core beliefs.

A negative core belief about yourself is usually based on faulty information (about you) that you were given as a child. Today, that data is seldom true

How Gifts change after Balancing

An example

After balancing your old compensating skills, the things you became very 'good at' to make up for your old core belief are now transformed into positive gifts, special skills you can share with others and to the world.

Before balancing - stuck with Old belief

I can't make things work

Old compensating skill:

I help others make things work, but somehow I can't do the same for myself.

After Balancing

Positive gifts for others:

I help other people fix things they can't fix by themselves

Inner gift - my positive compensating skill

My special ability is the way I show other people how to fix things and make things work.

Other inner gifts, to match appropriate core beliefs:

I help people feel valued;

I understand people;

I help people in pain;

I am loyal and faithful

Honour and appreciate your negative core belief's history

It is important to honour and appreciate the negative core belief's history, because it's also your history. In the way I describe in Book CBal-3, when you're doing your balancing you need to acknowledge the reasons why the negative core belief came into your life, reasons which underlie the absolute necessity for its existence when you were a child and then to acknowledge the need for its continued existence in your future.

From the very start when you or anyone who starts working with you and your negative core belief both you and your facilitator need to make it clear that:

* You both understand and accept these reasons and the necessity for the negative core belief to develop at that time as I have explained in this book.

and

* You are both ready to express your appreciation to your negative core belief for doing all that hard work back then to help protect you emotionally when you were a child.

Some of the most common reasons why negative core beliefs come into existence in our childhood include things like helping you "fit in with your family situation" or "making sense of what was happening to you as a child".

Make sure the negative core belief sees and understands that balancing is a positive process for it as well is for you.

The negative core belief needs reassuring that balancing also involves giving it (as a tired over-worked old belief) the opportunity to "share the load" with a matching opposite positive core belief.

As you do this everything about the negative core belief will start to change.

A Quick way to reduce the power of an old Core Belief

History has taught us that *not talking* about any kind of problem helps that problem grow stronger. On the other hand, talking about a problem usually reduces the power of that problem.

The more a problem increases our vulnerability, the more important it is to bring it out into the open, to talk about it. But too often those high vulnerability issues are the same ones that don't get brought up and aren't talked about.

An old negative core belief is a good example.

As you read on you will discover just how holding on to one old core belief can create the some of the worst problems in your life.

But those old beliefs are also closely related to your deepest vulnerability. So they remain hidden, not talked about and that means they grow and grow.

The good news. Once you name your old core belief and balance it, it begins to lose its power.

The more you talk about it openly the weaker it becomes.

Activity Sheet CB- 15 a

Keep this sheet private - Show it only to your therapist or counsellor or to close friends who will respect your confidentiality

Seventh Clue Part 1

Date __/__/__

Five 'gifts' from your old unbalanced core beliefs - Part 1

1. The first gift - making sense and fitting in.

Your unbalanced core belief helped you to "make sense of" what was happening to you in your family. What are some of the things that were going on in your family or happening around you or to you that *did not make sense to you* as a child and yet you somehow needed to have them "make sense"?

What did you need to change about your self as a child to be accepted or to fit in with your family? What were some of the ways that accepting and believing your unbalanced core belief then helped you to better "fit in" with your family? How did your old belief help you sit in your little chair with those old rules and old labels?

2. The second gift - your compensating skills helped you to be a success in the world.

Go back to Activity sheets CB- 12 and CB -13

List your compensating skills here, but describing them now as you see them as real "gifts" both inside for you and outside as they help you create gifts for other people.

3. The third gift is very special. - It's the personal power that comes with acknowledging your vulnerability and your imperfections. No need to hide them, no need to get triggered when things go wrong. Sometimes I do make mistakes, I can be wrong or not good enough (sometimes). That's normal. Without this gift you could not become an authentic mature grown-up. It's sometimes described as 'grown-up or adult humility' or in simple terms your ability to accept that as a grown-up you will always be vulnerable, always have a negative side to you, to accept your real faults, to acknowledge that you are wrong sometimes and that you do make mistakes. Your old core belief helped you to do these things but until now you may have been doing them in negative ways. Surprise, after balancing your two beliefs these same patterns become positive skills!
What are some of the skills like these that your old belief has given you that will now help you to be real and authentic and accept yourself and your grown-up vulnerability and reality?

Continued on the next page ....

Activity Sheet CB- 15 b

Keep this sheet private - Show it only to your therapist or counsellor or to close friends who will respect your confidentiality

Date __/__/__

Seventh Clue - Part 2

The five 'gifts' from your old unbalanced core beliefs - Part 2

4. Your fourth gift - empathy "I know how other people feel"; "I can support them when they make mistakes" "I can reassure them when they are troubled by their own old core beliefs." Plus your ability (only if you choose) to fit in with difficult situations and with difficult people.

This gift helps you connect with other people who share similar negative core beliefs or who make the same kind of mistakes you make. It also gives you the ability today to 'fit in' with difficult people or cope with difficult situations just as it helped you do that in your childhood. But, in future you can choose to do this, only when and if and how much, no longer because you give in to pressure or feel you 'have to'. You have not forgotten your childhood skills that came with your core belief.

Describe a time in the past when your fourth gift helped you connect with another person who needed empathy (rather than just giving sympathy which is not the same)

Describe a time when this fourth gift helped you fit in or be more comfortable with a difficult or unusual individual

Describe a recent time when this fourth gift helped you share empathy with a person who had a similar core belief to yours.

Continued on the next page ....

Activity Sheet CB- 15 c

Keep this sheet private - Show it only to your therapist or counsellor or to close friends who will respect your confidentiality

Date __/__/__

Seventh Clue - Part 2

The five 'gifts' from your old unbalanced core beliefs - *Part 3*

5. Your final and most important gift - the future gift, the gift of balance and the power to become the authentic person you were really meant to be.

The final gift is the gift of balance, the ability and the power that comes when you can sit between your negative belief and your positive belief and recognise how wonderful it is to have that balance back again. If you didn't still have your unbalanced core belief you couldn't do the balancing. It still has a place and will always have a place in your life.

How do you imagine your life will be different when you have connected with your positive belief and you can comfortably balance it with your old core belief?

What kind of feelings or emotions that you don't feel much at the moment, do you imagine you'll experience when you can sit comfortably between your positive and negative core beliefs and feel the balance?

What kind of positive beliefs could help you balance your old negative core belief?

What do you imagine might be some beautiful but hidden parts of your real, authentic personality, the person you were always meant to be, parts of you that have been hidden until now? Imagine how much easier it will be for you to reconnect with these parts of you after you have balanced your negative core belief with a positive one. That will be the most wonderful gift of all. What will your life be like in the future?

Your 'Core Issue'

Your Eighth clue

Like a flashing red neon sign' ..... and what it can attract into your life

Even when you cannot see your own negative core belief there are tell-tale signs that are so obvious to others that they could be described as like a flashing neon sign! These signs seem to attract the very people and events into our lives that will reinforce our negative belief so then it seems even more true than ever!

A core 'issue' is a kind of "big picture" summary of a Core Belief or a word that is directly associated with a Core Belief. It reflects one of the key life issues around which we all spend time and energy trying to live life and find solutions to the pain and problems that arise from having an unbalanced core belief.

Even when you cannot see your own negative core belief there are tell-tale signs that are so obvious to others that they could be described as like a flashing neon sign! These signs seem to attract the very people and events into our lives that will reinforce our negative belief so then it seems even more true than ever!

One of these signs directly connected to your negative core belief and your key life issues (see the list of key life issues on pages 67-68) is often your "core issue".

Once you have identified and named your core issue you find you can more easily identify and balance a Core Belief in a positive way.

If you have a negative core belief like *"I am always wrong"* or *'I can't get it right'* then your daily life, career and things that worry you most can all revolve all around issues that relate to right and wrong.

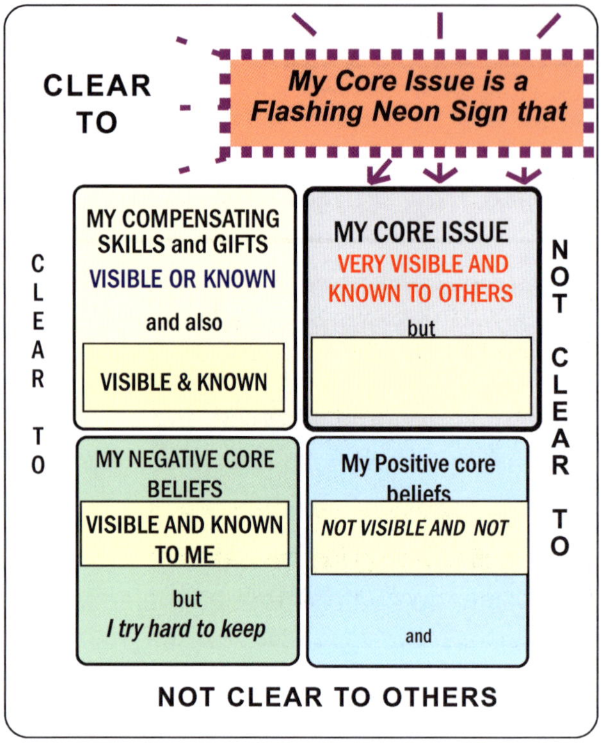

Other people will notice this more than you will.

You will be 'picked out'

You may work hard to compensate for this, but for example, it is likely that a trainer who can unconsciously 'see' your neon sign will pick you out as the one person in the room to answer a difficult question related to right and wrong issues.

Throughout your working life you may find yourself constantly attracted into legal areas or police work or both.

People who discover they have a core belief that they are so unlovable that they do not deserve a worthwhile partner are often amazed as they look back and notice how many partners they have had who all treated them like a doormat. (It is almost as if their neon sign only attracted that one kind of person.)

Examples:

My unbalanced core belief is 'I am not valuable'

My core issue is 'value'

My trigger words are 'no value' 'useless' or 'stupid'.

* * * * * *

My unbalanced core belief is 'I don't know what is real'

My core issues are 'reality' and 'knowing'

My trigger words are 'don't know' and 'no'

* * * * * *

My unbalanced core belief is 'I can't be myself'

My core issue is 'self' or 'myself'

My trigger word is 'selfish'

* * * * * *

My unbalanced core belief is 'I am worthless'

My positive core belief is 'I am worthwhile'

Unbalanced Negative Core beliefs and Core Issues

Unbalanced negative beliefs can be very different from person to person. Some are quite unique. Most core beliefs however are connected in a broad way with a sense of having lost your self worth or not being good enough:

Old Unbalanced Core Belief Patterns	Core Issues
1. Not good enough (I am not safe)	Security Safety
2. Not good enough (I don't belong)	Belonging, Nurture Self care
3. Not good enough (I have no value, I am worthless)	Self worth
4. Not good enough (I am powerless, I have no value)	Success Power Control
5. Not good enough (I am wrong, I am unsure)	Reality; Reason Knowing
6. Not good enough (My life is out of balance)	Balance Moderation
7. Not good enough (I don't exist; I am nothing)	Identity; Recognition
8. Not good enough (I am not real)	Self awareness
9. Not good enough (I am unlovable; left out; unwanted)	Love, Loved and Loving
10. Not good enough (I am defective)	Health; Self healing
11. Not good enough (I am not whole I have lost my spirit)	Wholeness; Spirit

Activity Sheet CB- 17

Keep this sheet private - Show it only to your therapist or counsellor or to close friends who will respect your confidentiality

Eighth Clue

Your core issue is a kind of short-hand way of recalling your core belief for example when you are triggered. Core issue words often turn up regularly in your conversation and are reflected in your daily goals and lifestyle. Issues can be positive or negative. Circle any words that are jumping out at you.

Positive Core Issues	*Opposite Core Belief Issue Words*
Hope	Hopeless
Trust	Distrust
Loved, Loving, Caring	Lonely, Alone
Happy Cheerful	Sad depressed
Joy	Joyless
Excitement, Anticipation	Bored
Surviving, Persisting	Folding
Thriving, Empowered, Strong	Powerless, Dis-empowered
Making things happen	Can't -do-it, Blocked
Surprised (happy)	Shocked, Confused
Impulsive, Rebelling	Controlled
Relaxed, Peaceful	Stressed
Balance	Unbalanced
Safe	Vulnerable
Confident	Scared, Anxious, Fearful
Belonging	Lonely, Alone, Lost
Proud to be me	Ashamed, Exposed
Not my problem	Guilty, Blamed , Over-responsible
Pain free	Hurting
Flying free	Trapped, Frustrated
Worth, Worthwhile ,Value	Worthless
Growing	Devastated, Losing
Healthy anger	Antagonistic, Blaming others
Other Positive Core issue words (for me)	Other old Core Belief feelings and Trigger words (for me)
_______ ______ _ ________	_______ _______ _ _______
____ __ ________ ____	_____ __ ________ ____

Core Issue Words and Trigger words - Examples

Are there just one or two words that summarise or reflect the thoughts behind your unbalanced or negative core beliefs? Core issue words ***(in italics below)*** are like this. These words turn up regularly in your daily conversation, your lifestyle, your key life issues and in your long term goals. They also point towards the nature of your 'core gifts', so they usually have a positive sound to them.

Trigger words (below not in italics) when you see or hear them, remind you of the negative side of your core issue and this reminder triggers some kind of intensity in you. The list below is by no means complete, but typical ***trigger words*** include: for example: 'value' 'knowing' 'worth' 'being' 'deserve' 'appreciation'.

Acceptable Acceptance
Acknowledgement
Action Acting Doing
Adequacy Adequate
Alone Lonely Lone
Always All the time
Anger Angry
Appreciation
Ashamed Shame Shameful
Availability
Aware Awareness
Bad Badly
Balance Balancing
Belong Belonging
Blame Guilt Wrong
Boundary Boundaries Barriers
Can Can't I can't
Caring Taking care Careful
Certain Uncertain Not sure
Clarity Clear
Clean Unclean Dirty
Connect Connection
Construction Reconstructing
Control Uncontrolled
Counting Count
Critic Criticised Critical
Dignity
Direct Direction Directing
Disgraceful Disgusted
Dumb Stupid
Effect Effective Effects
Enough Not good enough
Exist Existing Existence
Exposed
Facts Factual
Fail Failure Failing
Family Familiar
Fairness Fair Unfair
Faith Faithful
Fight Fighting
Fix Fix it up, Failure
Focus Focused
Freedom Free

Friend Friendly Friendship
Fullness
Future
Grow Growth Growing
Guilt Guilty Wrong Blamed
Good Good Enough
Harmony Peace Calm
Heal Healing
Help Helping Helpful Helpless
Honest Honesty Open
Hope Hopeful Hopeless
Ideal Ideals
Idiot Stupid
Ignored Ignorant
Important Importance
Inclusion Included
Individual Unique Special
Inferior Inferiority
Integrity
Justice Justifiable
Kind Kindness
Know Knowing Knowledge
Last Lasting Coming last
Like Likeable Liking
Link Linking Linkage
Love Loving Lovable
Loyal Loyalty
Matter Mattering
Mistake, Mistaken
Moderate Moderation
Natural Unnatural
Never Nobody
Nurture Nurturing
Open and Honest
Peace and Calm
Perfect
Place In place Right place
Possibility
Potent Potency Potential
Power Powerless Disempowering
Predictable Unpredictable
Real Reality Realistic
Recognition

Key Life Skills or Life Issues that we can't live without

Identity and Self-esteem
Boundary setting and holding
Reality and Noticing skills
Balancing Self Nurturing and Loving
Energy balancing, Moderation
Security skills *(Safety, Sanity, Self)*

Rely Reliable
Responsible Responsibility
Right Rights Get it Right
Safe Save Safety Saving
Self Self Worth Selfish
Sensitivity
Shame Shamed Shameful
Significance
Sound Soundness
Special Specialist
Spirit Spirituality
Strength Stable Strong Stability
Stupid Silly
Success Successful, unsuccessful
Superior Superiority
Support Supporting
Trust Trusting Trustworthy
Truth Truthful
Understanding Understood
Unique Individual
Unworthy unlovable
Useful Used Useless
Validation Valid
Value Valuable
Victim Victimised
Visible Visibility Vision Invisible
Vulnerable
Wanting Wanted Unwanted
Weak Weakness
Wholeness Whole
Work Working Can't Work
Worth Worthwhile Worthy
Worthless
Wrong Bad

Other Issues for You:

1. Circle any words that turn up regularly in your conversation with friends or in discussions with your therapist. Circle words you think might reflect the nature of your deepest issues about life. Add other words that come to your mind that might also be a part of your core issue.
2. Underline any of the words that irritate or annoy you, create an uncomfortable feeling or a sense of vulnerability

Activity Sheet CB- 18

Keep this sheet private - Show it only to your therapist or counsellor or to close friends who will respect your confidentiality

Eighth Clue

Date __/__/_

Identifying your core issue

Your core issue is a kind of short-hand way of recalling your core beliefs when you need to in a hurry, for example when you are triggered. It's better if your core issue has a positive sound to it, for example: 'value' - 'knowing' - 'worth' - 'being' - 'appreciation'. Core issue words often turn up regularly in your conversation and are reflected in your daily goals and lifestyle.

1. Circle any of the words on the last few pages that you think might be close to your core issue or that might reflect the nature of your deepest issues about life. The list of words on the previous two pages is far from complete - please add any other words here that come to your mind that you feel might be a part of your core issue:

   ----

2. Underline any of the words on the last few pages, that turn up regularly in your conversation with friends or in discussions with people (or your counsellor / therapist) about your life

3. Add any other words not on those lists but words that keep coming into your mind and that relate more closely to the most important issues in your life, or trigger your feelings.

   ----

4. My 'trigger words' - the words that cause me to react with some intensity when I hear them (or see them) include ....

   ----

5. If one word or one word group is close to your core issue you may feel an immediate sense of deep understanding described as 'resonance'. Which words give you this feeling?

   ----

6. I think my core issue might be ________ *(one or two words only)* ________

Examples:

My unbalanced core belief is 'I am not valuable'

My core issue is 'value'

My trigger words are 'no value' 'useless' or 'stupid'.

* * * * * *

My unbalanced core belief is 'I don't know what is real'

My core issues are 'reality' and 'knowing'

My trigger words are 'don't know' and 'no'

* * * * * *

My unbalanced core belief is 'I can't be myself'

My core issue is 'self' or 'myself'

My trigger word is 'selfish'

* * * * * *

My unbalanced core belief is 'I am worthless'

My positive core belief is 'I am worthwhile'

My core issue is 'worth'

My trigger words are 'deserve' and 'worthless'

Every day of your life . . . . Resonance

Every day of your life your core beliefs and their predicting, forecasting supporting beliefs will help you 'discover' evidence that seems to prove that they are really true.

Each day they will help you to have new experiences that 'prove' they are real and help you avoid experiences that would make those beliefs seem less true.

Each day they will attract people into your life (and attract you to people) who will help 'prove' that the belief is still true, while keeping you away from others who might make it seem less true.

Each day they will help you observe outcomes or results arising from your thoughts and actions that help 'prove' the belief is true while you totally ignore other results that would prove it was untrue.

It will be there in the background too

Resonance describes the way a big brass gong continues vibrating and giving off a deep sound for some time after it was struck. It's a kind of echo and core issues also have a pattern of echoing in our life in ways that have little to do with the actual belief.

Ten years before I first found out about core beliefs I had decided to get a personalised number plate for my car. I didn't have the faintest idea that my old negative would turn out to be "I have No Value."

My initials are JBN so that part was easy. Then I had to choose a two digit number to follow. What number did I select? Not number one '01' which was available. Instead I opted for "00" Double zero, nothing, no value.

Thirty years later I still have that number plate JBN-00 even though I no longer accept the old belief. That's an example of core belief resonance, an action that only the vaguest background connection to the core issue and yet which echos it strongly in places where other peopele can see it!.

Most readers will be familiar with this story. I have included it here because it reminds me so much of the way our negative core beliefs cause us to reject the positive messages and accept the negative ones, as I explain throughout this book.
The more you feed your negative core belief the stronger it gets. The only way to balance it is to feed your positive core belief as well.

An Old Cherokee Lesson

A wise old Cherokee is teaching his grandson about life. *"There is a fight that is always going on inside me,"* he explained to the boy.

"It is a terrible fight and it is between two wolves. One wolf is negative - he is anger, envy, sorrow, regret, greed, arrogance, self-pity, guilt, resentment, inferiority, lies, false pride, superiority, and ego."

However, he continued,

"The other wolf is good - he is joy, peace, love, hope, serenity, humility, kindness, benevolence, empathy, generosity, truth, compassion, and faith.

The same fight is going on inside you - and inside every other person, too."

The grandson thought about it for a minute and then asked his grandfather,

"Which wolf inside me will win?"

The old Cherokee replied,

"The one you feed."

Any resemblance to any actual individual is not intended. These fictional case studies have been created only for training. However do not be too surprised if you see something of yourself in these fictitious characters.

Case Study - *Fred* Voted Most Likely (not) to Succeed

Marketing consultant, Fred in the past has often displayed amazing success and set outstanding levels of achievement when motivated. Once he received a national award as a Multi-million Dollar Sales Achiever.

Even before turning 21 Fred was a runner up for a state award as Young Achiever of the Year. As a management consultant he has helped so many of his clients achieve success.

Fred still tries very hard but somehow the end result of each new change in his life is another failure or an increased loss. Two failed marriages.

Now in his mid 60's Fred has very little left in the way of assets. He suffers from severe backache problems which doctors seem unable to fix.

Each time he fails, Fred blames the people around him, bosses, colleagues, customers, the government, the media, his parents, his partners, his children.

Fred gets very upset if anyone who is close to him suggests that he might in some way be partly responsible for his problems or his pain and argues strongly, presenting "evidence" to prove that he is not in any way at fault.

Childhood history

Constantly criticised by both parents who told Little Fred that he would never amount to anything. Compared to his older sibling who was the one hailed as the "brother who will be a success" (The older brother is now bankrupt and an alcoholic).Fred attained very high marks throughout high school but his parents refused to support him when he wanted to go on to University.

However, after his second marriage break-up, Fred did make it to university as an evening student and gained a Master's Degree in Business Management with a very high pass.

> ***Wanting others to feel your pain usually means you want them to fix it for you.***
> ***When you feel it by yourself, you can heal it by yourself***

Unbalanced Core Belief Checklist

1. Do these signs point to the possibility Fred might have an unbalanced core belief?

* Too often things that Fred does or that people do with Fred seem to go wrong.
Yes / No / not sure

* Certain words, actions or events seem to 'trigger' him into a strong reaction or F patterns that are intense and use a lot of energy.
Yes / No / not sure

* These patterns are repeated regularly.
Yes / No / not sure

* He wishes he could change those repeated patterns but doesn't seem able to.
Yes / No / not sure

* Fred may have physical body pain or a deep emotional wounding or both that hurt him deep inside.)

Yes / No / not sure

Q 1 Total Yes ___ Total No ___

Q.2 What are other people doing or saying to Fred just before he starts to over-react?

_ _

_ _

Q 3. What are two of his more obvious trigger events?

_ _ _ _ _ _ _ _ _ _ _ _ _ _ _ _ _ _

_ _

FIRST CLUE What are two of his repeated over-reactions or F patterns, when he is triggered? (see pp 12-14 for list).

_ _

_ _

SECOND CLUE What does Fred try to get other people to change? For example the things they do or say to him (and he has little success).

_ _

_ _

What are some problems Fred sees as outside

of him might really be more inside him?

_ _

THIRD CLUE He makes negative forecasts or predictions about how people are going to treat him or what he expects people will say to him. What might be two of his predicting, forecasting or similar supporting beliefs? _

Unbalanced Negative core beliefs - general patterns

Negative beliefs or feelings about myself:	Bottom line Issues
1. Not good enough (I am not safe)	Security Safety
2. Not good enough (I don't belong)	Belonging, Nurture Self care
3. Not good enough (I have no value, I am worthless)	Self worth
4. Not good enough (I am powerless, I have no value)	Success Power Control
5. Not good enough (I am wrong, I am unsure)	Reality; Reason Knowing
6. Not good enough (My life is out of balance)	Balance Moderation
7. Not good enough (I don't exist; I am nothing)	Identity; Recognition
8. Not good enough (I am not real)	Self awareness
9. Not good enough (I am unlovable; left out; unwanted)	Love, Loved and Loving
10. Not good enough (I am defective)	Health; Self healing
11. Not good enough (I am not whole I have lost my spirit)	Wholeness; Spirit

FOURTH CLUE What are some of Fred's most successful or most powerful compensating skills (one of the five gifts from his core belief). As a managemnent consultant what did he give as gifts to others? Remember that although compensating skills work quite well for a start, especially in Fred's workplace, sooner or later they start to lose their power.

_ _

Inner Detective Guide

1. First Clue - triggered reactions

Triggered over-reactions are the most obvious clues that an unbalanced core belief is 'at work' inside Fred or in another person.

Advanced Detective work

Each of these sections will give you one particular sign, clue or pointer to help you identify Fred's old Core Belief.

2. Second clue- Fred thinks power is in other people and outside of him.

3. Third Clue - Fred's Prophecies, Predictions and Forecasts about what other people will do to him

4. Fourth Clue - Fred's Compensating gifts/ skills.

5. Fifth Clue - Fred's Family History

6. Sixth Clue - Fred has trouble accepting success

7. Seventh Clue - Fred's Five Core Gifts

8. Eighth Clue - Fred's core issue word

FIFTH CLUE Can you see a connection between what's happening inside Fred, his trigger events, his compensating skills and his childhood history? Connection :

_ _

SIXTH CLUE What happens to Fred when he actually achieves success?

_ _

Seventh and Eighth CLUES What else have you noticed about Fred that could help identify his Negative Core Belief? What might be his 'core issue' word?

_ _

PUT THE EIGHT CLUES TOGETHER

When you're ready refer to the General Core Belief pattern list (above) or better still, go to the long list of different beliefs on pages **26-29** in this book.

Choose one or more negative beliefs that match the eight clues and that you think Fred might be holding inside him. _

Note: There are many "correct" answers. No wrong ones.

If you are feeling worried about being "wrong" could it be your old core belief at work?

Not everything that goes wrong is a Negative Core Belief problem

Working with your own negative core belief is powerful and positive. But not all our problems can be traced back to just this one issue.

Other factors also lead to negative reactions or life patterns. They could be connected to a Core Belief or they may be completely independent.

1. Repeated patterns of Self-Defeating behaviour (RSDP)

These are highly significant patterns, and they can be set up by an unbalanced core belief, or on the other hand they can help to set up the belief.

I explain about RSDP on my website.

www.voice-dialogue-inner-self-awareness.com/RSDP.html

If you Google "RSDP." you will see other websites on topics that are not Repeated Self-Defeating Patterns but my web page is:

www.voice-dialogue-inner-self-awareness.com/RSDP.html

2. A personal history that includes severe or repeated trauma or abuse as a child.

See my web page:

http://www.voice-dialogue-inner-self-awareness.com/dtd.html

also my website:

www.love-your-inner-child.com

3. Adverse Childhood Experiences ACE

Not all bad childhood experiences are classed as trauma or abuse but if they are negative and if they happen regularly they can have a serious effect in adult life. The higher your ACE score the more lots of things go wrong in life.

See my web page:

http://www.ACE.realme1.com

4. Getting stuck in an addictive cycle.

See my web page:

www.voice-dialogue-inner-self-awareness.com/addictions16.html

"Money, time, relationships, professional skills, family, everything has been reorganised so that it can be better used to distance me from my pain, my vulnerability and my fear of my negative beliefs getting any worse than they already are.
In doing so I also distance myself from the love or power or freedom or happiness or wealth or health or safety or whatever I am desperately seeking"

(Nikki Nemerouf)

Eight Clues that help Identify a Core Belief

1. *Your triggered F Reactions*
2. *Your old "Power is Outside of me" rule*
3. *Your Prophecies Predictions Forecasts*
4. *Gifts you give away to Compensate*
5. *Your Family History*
6. *Discomfort accepting compliments/success*
7. *Your Core Gifts*
8. *Your Core issue*

Other False Beliefs that Stand Behind a Core Belief

1. **Thinking long and hard or debating with others about my core belief might uncover positive evidence** that could help disprove my core belief. *(False)*

2. **My negative core belief gives me amazing powers to predict, prophesise and forecast the kind of negative things other people will do and say to me.** That helps me prepare myself for them before they happen. *(False)*

3. **No matter how good things are some days there will always be bad days to follow.** I must not get my hopes up too much. *(False)*

4. **Again and again, things will happen and people will say and do things to me that make me feel I am really not good enough or powerless or that there is something terribly wrong with me**. Each time that confirms my negative core belief and makes it more real than ever. (False)

5. **When people remind me about my core belief that way I am entitled to have very strong reactions** (my triggered F reactions). That will discourage them from doing it again. *(False)*

6. **Hiding the pain of my negative core belief from other people will discourage them** from coming up with even more evidence to support it. *(False)*

7. **Who I am and how much I matter is determined by other people, not by me.** So the only way to disprove a core belief is to get lots of evidence from other people. I cannot do it myself. *(False)*

8. **Some people who live and work with me have evidence that could help disprove my negative core belief.** They know ways that might stop me feeling 'not good enough'. Those people could help me if they wanted to but most times they don't even try. Meanwhile, other people seem to enjoy coming up with more evidence to make my negative belief stronger. *(False)*

9. **It is unwise to trust people or events at those times when they try to help by suggesting my core beliefs are not true.** They are usually only after something from me. On the other hand I need to believe people and events whenever they make my old core belief seem more believable. *(False)*

10. **However, working hard will impress other people** and should encourage them to come up with the evidence I need from them to disprove my core belief. *(False)*

If you have now completed the Core Belief Activity sheets numbered CB-1 to CB-21 in this book you'll almost certainly be ready to identify your own unique Unbalanced Old Core belief.

If you are still not sure now, then please e-mail me bligh4@growingaware.com and I'll help. Your first live session on line is always free.

Yes - you can have positive core beliefs too

"Children who consistently feel, valued, nurtured, protected and encouraged have a positive core belief that they are worthwhile. The memory of having been loved and supported remains a reliable resource, a shield against the harsh realities of life." (Jack Morin)

Those who did not get that kind of family protection had to adapt to survive and cope as best they could. This is where the development of unbalanced negative beliefs actually assisted at the time.

Those beliefs helped the small child 'fit' into their unbalanced negative family system by encouraging the development of new patterns and supporting beliefs that led to *'better'* ways of doing things (ways that seemed 'better' because they suited the family rather than the child).

Once your positive grown up self aware system replaces the missing nurturing and protection, you will find you very seldom need a negative belief to 'make sense of' or help you fit in with the negativity in the world around you.

Activity Sheet CB- 19

Keep this sheet private - Show it only to your therapist or counsellor or to close friends who will respect your confidentiality

Date __/__/_

Checklist - Getting Ready to Name Your old unbalanced core belief

*Go back and check your activity sheets. If you notice any similar points, recurring themes or just words that are repeated in what you have written on your activity sheets please note them on this sheet. That recurring word or theme will reflect your **core issue** and give you a key to your unbalanced core belief.*

Signs and General Indicators (Sheet CB-1) Any similar points or repeated words?

____

____

First Clue: Out of all my reactions (My Triggers and my Trigger Events (Activity Sheets CB-2 CB4a, CB4b, CB5) my highest scoring or most common *individual* 'F' reactions. Look for any similar points or repeated words.

F. _ Score ____ _______________ *(words)* ________

F. _ Score ____ _______________ *(words)* ________

F. _ Score ____ _______________ *(words)* ________

F. _ Score ____ _______________ *(words)* ________

Second Clue: Outside of Me Intentions (Sheets CB-6; CB-7;CB-8 Any similar themes or repeated words?

____

____

Third Clue: My Predicting, Forecasting or Supporting beliefs (Sheet CB- 9; CB-10) Any similar themes, repeated words?

____

____

Fourth Clue: My Compensating Skills and the gifts I give to other people (Sheet CB- 11; CB12) Any similar similar patterns or repeated words or themes?

____

____

Fifth Clue: My Childhood History (Sheet CB- 13) Any similar points or repeated words or patterns?

____

____

Activity Sheet CB- 20

Keep this sheet private - Show it only to your therapist or counsellor or to close friends who will respect your confidentiality

Checklist - Part Two

Date __/__/_

Sixth Clue: My discomfort accepting success, receiving praise or appreciation (CB- 14) Any similar points or repeated words?

Seventh Clue: My five Core Gifts (Sheet CB-15 and CB-16) Any similar themes or repeated words?

Eighth Clue: My Core Issue words (Sheet CB-17; CB-18) Any similar themes or repeated words?

Are there any other similar topics or repeated words about you or your belief that now come into your mind?

What do you believe your old negative Core Belief **has cost you** over the years?

Any other words or thoughts *about who you are or who you are not ?*

Activity Sheet CB- 21 part A

Keep this sheet private - Show it only to your therapist or counsellor or to close friends who will respect your confidentiality

Date __/__/__

It's good to name your old unbalanced core belief

The more often you name it, the less often it can hurt you!

Every core belief has a connection with your sense of self-worth or not being good enough, but your own beliefs about yourself can be quite different from other people's because yours, in the past, provided *you* with a framework that helped you interpret and understand the most painful experiences you have had to face in *your* life.

If you feel ready, write down what you think could be some of your own most familiar ***negative*** statements about yourself. Do not think too much about this. Write freely, using the first words that come into your head. The suggestions below are only examples. Use any phrase that comes to mind:

I AM NOT GOOD ENOUGH BECAUSE ________ *(negative reason)* ________

____

I AM NOT ________ *(negative statement)* ________

I AM ________ *(negative statement)* ________

I DON'T ________ *(negative statement)* ________

I CAN'T BECAUSE I ________ *(negative reason)* ________

I AM ALWAYS ________ *(negative statement)* ________

I NEVER ________ *(negative statement)* ________.

EVERYTHING THAT I ________ *(negative statement)* ________

NOTHING THAT I ________ *(negative statement)* ________

IF I CAN'T ________ *THEN* ________ *(negative result)* ________

I WISH I COULD - ________ *(positive wish)* ________ BUT I CAN'T *BECAUSE* ________

________ *(negative statement)* ________

I DON'T DESERVE TO ________ *(positive wish)* ________

I AM AFRAID THAT I ________________________

I AM AFRAID THAT IF I ________________ .*THEN .I* ________________

________________ another *(negative statement)* ________________

That's not all. This list continues on the next page

Activity Sheet CB- 21 Part B

THINGS I DON'T LIKE ABOUT MYSELF ------ *(negative descriptions)* --------

------ --------- -------------- - -- ----------

------------- - -------- ------------- - -- -------- --

------------- - -------- ------------- - -- -------- --

------------- - -------- ------------- - -- -------- --

2. Underline the two negative phrases from both pages that you try hardest to hide or prevent others seeing in you
3. Circle the two negative phrases from both pages that seem most powerful, or that have the most control over your life
4. Now re-word those four negative statements in a more direct form. Try to use fewer words and shorter words. Who do you feel you are or aren't?

This time, make sure what you write is about *who or what YOU are or are not* - rather than what you do or don't do.

Avoid anything that refers to other people. Example: you might write *'I am not lovable'* rather than *'People don't love me'* or *'Nobody will ever love me'*

------------- - -------- ------------- - -- --------

------------- - -------- ------------- - -- --------

------------- - -------- ------------- - -- --------

------------- - -------- ------------- - -- --------

------------- - -------- ------------- - -- --------

5. Remind yourself that as soon as you identify your unbalanced beliefs, you can start to balance them with your own real and positive beliefs that are waiting for you to claim them. Remind yourself that the more often you 'name' your old unbalanced or negative beliefs *the less often they can hurt you!*

Some Positive and well Balanced Core Beliefs

Positive beliefs or feelings about myself:	Life Issues
1. I am good enough (I feel safe; I can look after myself)	Security Safety
2. I am good enough (I belong; I don't feel too vulnerable)	Belonging, Nurture Self care
3. I am good enough (I have value, I am worthwhile)	Self worth
4. I am good enough (I have a sense of my personal power; Whatever I need, I can usually find)	Success Power Control
5. I am good enough (I am confident; I make sense)	Reality; Reason Knowing
6. I am good enough (My life is in balance)	Balance Moderation
7. I am good enough (I am me; I am who I am meant to be)	Identity; Recognition
8. I am good enough (I am aware and grown up and real)	Self awareness
9. I am good enough (I am lovable; I am included)	Love, Loved and Loving
10. I am good enough (I am healthy and whole)	Health; Self healing
11. I am good enough (I feel whole; connected with my inner spirit)	Wholeness; Spirit

Activity Sheet CB- 22

Keep this sheet private - Show it only to your therapist or counsellor or to close friends who will respect your confidentiality

Date __/__/_

Inventory - Getting Ready to Embrace your Positive Core beliefs

Taking an inventory of what your unbalanced core belief has cost you over the years will help motivate you to find, name and embrace it with your Positive Core Belief and then balance the two beliefs

1. **The more times you state your old unbalanced core belief, the less it can hurt you.** Write it down again here. (if you have more than one belief write them all down) in whatever way that makes it/them seem clearest to you. Try saying it/them out loud . (You may want to try writing it/them in a couple of different ways to help find the wording that seems most powerful in its effect on you and your life.

2. If you have any sense of deep pain that you associate with your old unbalanced core beliefs write a few words about that pain or loss. What does this pain feel like? When you're triggered, where do you feel it in your body? (This is your core pain)

3. What are some examples of what your old unbalanced core beliefs cost you in terms of:
   Career or financial losses
   Lost chances of success
   Health losses
   Lost opportunities
   Relationship losses
   Other losses

4. What are the usual end results or outcomes (for you) at those times when you let your old automatic responses like your typical 'F' reaction patterns control your life and your relationships?

5. Think about the first of the five 'gifts' from your old negative beliefs *(Sheet CB-10*) How did they help you?

7. What really useful compensating skills did these beliefs help you develop? *(Sheets CB-8)*

8.. Which of these compensating skills do you expect to be most useful after you have balanced your beliefs?

9.. Were there any other positive outcomes for which you could thank your unbalanced core beliefs today?

Activity Sheet CB- 23

Keep this sheet private - Show it only to your therapist or counsellor or to close friends who will respect your confidentiality

Identifying your positive belief

Date __/__/_

For a start let's see if you can find some positive words to say about yourself that will help you get a sense of what your Positive Core Belief might look, feel or sound like

1. Usually a positive core belief is not just the positive verbal opposite of the negative one . As explained in this book, finding the right words for your positive belief can take some time. But for the moment see if you can come up with a few descriptive words to reflect the kind of positive energy that would help to balance your negative belief.
The statements need to be about YOU - not what you believe you can do for other people.
Don't worry about getting the words 'right'

2. Now see if you can express your positive belief in a more direct form - using shorter words. The statements need to be about who YOU are - not what you do or believe you can do for other people. Rewrite the statement a few times to see which one feels and sounds the most positive and the most comfortable inside you.

I am good enough because I ....

I am good enough because I ....

I am powerful because I ....

I am a success because ....

I am ....

Preparing for Your Balancing Session
Six Steps

The more preparations you make the better. I developed the Core Detective approach to help speed up your Core Belief processes. It works, but only if you follow it through like a good detective.

A Fast n' Easy Fix - cannot work

Sometimes a reader will contact me two days after they received this book, saying *"I know my Old Core Belief and I'm ready to balance it!"* ......

But when I ask if they've completed the activity sheets they say they been too busy. Having picked out a likely belief from the list of 200 they would like to skip the Activity sheets and zip straight to some kind of (imaginary) fast fix. Sorry, but it can't happen that way.

I have yet to see one of these people even identify their real core belief at that stage, let alone be really ready to balance it. It's a bit like a detective rounding up one of the usual suspects and pinning the crime on them with enough evidence. *It can't work.*

Balancing the front half a belief - waste of time

I have had other readers contact me a week after they received their books and say *"I've completed Activity sheets CB-1 to CB-5. Can I do the Balancing now?"*

We can try, but the usual problem here is that they have only identified the front half the belief, for example *"I can't."* when after completing the rest of the Activity sheets they would have discovered their Core Belief was really *"I can't succeed."* Their core issue was not "can't" but *"success."*

That's why it is important to put the time in and to identify all eight clues before you begin a balancing session that's going to work.

Balancing the front half of a belief is OK for practice but not much help because it doesn't balance the real issue. You end up needing to do it again anyway later on. An early balancing session may be useful for you to experience what it's like sitting between the two energy states. At least you are getting away from trying to think it through rationally, which won't fix it anyway.

On the other hand quite often a hard working and usually a busy reader will contact me ten days after they received their books and explain *"I've completed all the Activity sheets CB-1 to CB-23. I have identified two different beliefs. What do I do next?"*

That's when we are ready to begin what I like to refer to as their "Balancing Ceremony"

It is so important from the start to understand why your negative core beliefs come into existence, to name them, honour them and accept them rather than treating the negative core belief as if it was a "bad" or shameful part.

Why you need to state your negative core belief clearly in a few short words

Balancing can't start until you have identified one or more of your negative core beliefs. That's the purpose of the Activity sheets **to help you identify at least one specific negative core belief.**

After you have identified your belief try if you to put into a few words, short clear distinct words. If you need help with naming it just refer to the 200 examples in this book pages 26 - 29.

If you are not clear enough on exactly what your is core belief it is better to go back and repeat the Activity sheets until you are fairly sure that you can state it clearly.

Keep in mind that a core belief is always an "I am not good enough because I am .... or "Because I am not.... or something similar. Any statement about other people like "Nobody loves me." is only a supporting belief. It's not the one you need to work with when you are balancing.

One of the ways that the negative core belief maintains power over you is to remain unknown and unnamed while working in the background to disempower you or block your energy.

During the balancing process you will not only name the belief over and over but you will also become much more familiar with it so that it is can never be hidden from you again.

If you were to do nothing else just becoming consciously aware of your negative core belief and naming it will make a significant difference.

PREPARATION STEP 1

Write your negative core belief out on a sheet of paper using clear descriptive words perhaps beginning with the phrase "I am not good enough because ....

Make sure that your negative belief statement is worded in a way that expresses a negative belief about you not a forecast or prediction about what other people might do to you as a consequence of the way they see you and your negative core belief.

If you need a reminder of the wording go back to Personal Activity sheet CB-21

PREPARATION STEP 2

Reassure your negative core belief about its future

You and the person assisting or facilitating the balancing need to gain the support of the negative core belief before you start going out to meet the positive core belief.

Most core beliefs are like intelligent sub-personalities. They worry about you. They often worry that the positive belief might come in, take over and kick them out.

They know that the end result would be that you would be just as out of balance as before but in the opposite direction.

As I explained at the start, inner selves or sub-personalities worry a lot and they often share that worry with all the other parts of you, and then all of you feels worried. In the case of a negative core belief sub personality one of their worries is that they are going to be *"got rid of"*. As I have explained in each book in this series it can't happen but the negative core belief may not be so sure.

So right at the start before you begin to talk with them about balancing they need to be reassured that this cannot happen. You need to reassure the negative core belief that what is going to take place in the next few minutes does not involve any idea of "getting rid of it".

One of the reasons why it's very important to go back and find out where your old belief came from, is that this is the only way you are going to understand why something so completely untrue could have become so firmly embedded within you as an "unquestioned truth".

The second reason is to do with the process as you balance your negative core belief self. You can't get rid of that belief. It is hard-wired into your brain cells and in fact trying to get rid of it only locks it in even more firmly. But you can balance **it.**

No sackings No redundancies

However, before you can balance it with a matching positive believe you do have to do something first and that is to reassure the negative belief that it is not going to be subtly done away with by the positive belief. (Negative beliefs are a living part of you and yes they talk to you regularly and yes they are worried about being sacked or made redundant.

They must be reassured that this is not going to happen and in fact cannot happen to them.

Honouring the Gifts

That's why a very important part of the process is described as "honouring" the gifts that the negative core belief gave you, in your childhood.

First let's remind ourselves where negative core beliefs come from

In childhood, adapting and taking on negative core beliefs does have some real advantages. **It may have been** our negative core beliefs that helped us to disown or hide some beloved natural parts of us because they were stopping us fitting in with our family. This we had to do, so that we could gain the approval and nurturing we so badly wanted from our families.

In my case, as a child, a negative belief that *'I have no value'* helped me to grow up and become a 'little adult' very rapidly because there was no place for a playful child in my work driven family. Only people who could help share the load of the daily work on the farm were of any value.

This belief was what my parents demanded of me before I was accepted as a fitting member of the family and it was my negative belief that helped me to complete my adaption from a child to an unpaid farm labourer by around eight years of age. In the eyes of my family I had now become valuable, not as John but as an extra member of the workforce.

In dealing with core beliefs like these in later life we need to acknowledge that they did serve this essential purpose at that time. They were not 'bad' or 'wrong' just very pragmatic about helping us change things about us we did not want to change but which we *had to change* to survive to gain acceptance in our family.

Why the gift of balance so important

Understanding the gifts may help explain why we all need to balance our old negative beliefs with positive ones, rather than just try throw the negative ones out. To lose the old belief would leave us feeling *too positive* and in the end just as unbalanced, only in the opposite direction. With no negative belief we would find it hard to recognise that we sometimes do make mistakes, to acknowledge this openly and do something practical about fixing them.

Let's suppose for example that my positive belief had became over-developed and my negative core belief self became too weak. That would mean I would be out of balance and going around making a fuss about how wonderful I was giving my gifts away. Before long I would be a pain in the butt for people around me (who would then stop valuing me).

Maintaining and embracing my old negative core belief allows me to maintain a nice flexible balance between my adult humility and my sense of having true value, whether or not other people recognize it. That's the fifth gift and I couldn't have that gift if I didn't continue to use and embrace my old negative core belief to help me maintain a proper balance with my positive one.

That's why I continue to emphasise how important it is that you are careful not to put yourself in the hands of a counsellor or psychotherapist who suggests they can help you "remove", or "get rid of" your negative core belief.

Not only will they fail but they can do real damage while they are trying.

Honouring and appreciating your negative core belief's history

It is important to honour and appreciate the negative core belief's history, because it's also your history. In the same way as I described in Book CBal-3. When you are doing advanced balancing you need to acknowledge the reasons why the negative core belief came into your life, reasons which underlie the absolute necessity for its existence when you were a child and then to acknowledge the need for its continued existence in your future.

From the very start when you or anyone who starts working with you and your negative core belief both you and your facilitator need to make it clear that:

* You both understand and accept these reasons and the necessity for the negative core belief to develop at that time as I have explained in this book.

and

* You are both ready to express your appreciation to your negative core belief for doing all that hard work back then to help protect you emotionally when you were a child.

Explain some of the most common reasons why negative core beliefs come into existence in childhood.

Those reasons include things like helping you "fit in with your family situation" or "making sense of what was happening to you as a child".

You might like to go back and read the closing paragraphs of the story *"The Case of the Stolen Self-esteem"* in Book CB-6 to help you appreciate this.

The next preparation steps will help to reassure your negative core belief that "it's going to be alright" before you start.

As you do this everything about the negative core belief will start to change.

Make sure the negative core belief sees and understands that balancing is a positive process for it as well is that you.

It is equally important to reassure the negative core belief that balancing is also a positive process which involves giving it as a tired over-worked old belief the opportunity to "share the load" with a matching opposite positive core belief.

This demonstrates that you are hoping to balance your two beliefs in a positive way and encourages support from your negative core belief before you start going out to meet your positive core belief.

Before you continue, make certain that the negative core belief is sufficiently reassured to accept the idea of sharing the responsibility of looking after you with a positive belief with lots of balancing.

This is why the next preparation steps are so important.

PREPARATION STEP 3

Write the list of your own five or more special gifts on a separate sheet of paper.

Remember to honour the five gifts from your negative core belief.

To add to this positive approach you also need to name, honour and acknowledge each of the "gifts" that you have gained or derived just by having the negative core belief in your life.

This may seem difficult to understand at first but it is essential before you can balance your negative and positive belief. You will have identified yours when you completed the Activity sheets in Book CBal-2.

Honour the five gifts from your negative core belief.

Recognising the negative core belief and the role that it played in your early childhood helping you to fit in with your family was the first gift. Your compensating skills are the second gift. As well there are other gifts.

The last and most important gift of all is the gift of balance. This is the most important gift of all because it will help you develop more balance in your life.

You can't have balance if you don't have both a negative and positive core belief. As well as the main gifts, remember that other gifts include increasing your empathy for other people who have a similar negative core belief.

If you need a reminder of the wording go back to Activity sheets CB 15 and CB-16

PREPARATION STEP 4

List your positive compensating skills on a separate sheet of paper

One of your gifts was your wonderful and very important "Compensating skills".

These skills are usually related to your chosen line of work, your career, or your profession. The reason why you developed the skills, as explained in this book and more in Book CBal-6 is directly related to your negative core belief because they presented you with a way of compensating for that belief. Now your knowledge and acceptance of these skills is going to help you to balance your beliefs as well.

At this point you're almost ready to start the core belief separating and balancing process following the scripts and guidelines in the next few pages.

PREPARATION STEP 5

If you have already identified one or more of your Positive Core beliefs write them down as well

If you are not yet clear about the wording make a summary of whatever notes you have already made about what you think might be your positive core belief. Activity sheets CB- 15 to CB-18

However, if you don't have any idea of what your positive core belief is at this stage don't worry.

PREPARATION STEP 6

Remind yourself and your inner child that this is grown-up's work . Your Inner Child must be reassured that it is not expected to participate in the session.

Balancing will only work if you are able to work the process from your Grown-up Self Aware Self, or as I often describe it, your STAR and WING zones. If your Inner Child believes he or she will have to do even some of the balancing ***it will not work.***

Learning to work from your central grown up self-aware position will allow you to move freely between the two beliefs, to balance them and finally developing and strengthening each of the two beliefs, preparing them for their role working together in the future.

Practicing your skill as the grown-up self aware part that takes charge of the balancing process.

Later on when you are in your WING or your SAGE zones you discover how to adjust the strength of each belief, positive and negative, according to how much each one is needed to deal most effectively with each changing situation.

I will explain more then about what you do after you have separated and connected with your opposite balancing energy, your positive core belief.

At that point you can start to communicate directly with your positive core belief self and then discover how to place your self aware grown-up parts firmly in the middle between the two opposite beliefs.

The final step is learning to adjust the strength of the positive and negative belief in a different way rather than moving from chair to chair.

You and the person assisting you are now ready to start balancing.

Activity Sheet CB- 24

Keep this sheet private - Show it only to your therapist or counsellor or to close friends who will respect your confidentiality

Date __/__/__

Embracing your Positive Beliefs

One way to start making use of your positive belief is to begin making changes in the way you deal with life's problems especially other people, things or events that trigger your old F reactions

1. Next time you're triggered, what could you *think to yourself or tell yourself*, that would be new, novel or different?

2. Next time you're triggered, *what could you now say* that would just be new, novel or different?

3. Next time you're triggered, *what could you actually do*, that would just be new, novel or different? (Changing from automatic to manual control of your reactions.)

4. One of the main changes that you notice after you have identified and embraced your positive belief is the way they can counter-balance the energy of the old negative belief, the gift of balance. What kinds of positive changes do you think having that kind of balance might mean for you ?

IT ISN'T IMPORTANT what you choose to think, say or try, or how well these changes work, as long as they are *different from* your old automatic 'F' reaction patterns. What is important is that you are showing the world that your automatic repetitive over reaction F patterns no longer have control over you or about how you think and feel or what you say to other people.

Each time you're triggered, you now have the power to ***choose your own response.***

Activity Sheet CB- 25

Keep this sheet private - Show it only to your therapist or counsellor or to close friends who will respect your confidentiality

Date __/__/_

Honouring the real "I am." The natural, authentic you, that you really are

Once you stop being driven by the negative side of your old unbalanced beliefs you begin to experience the positive nature of your real and natural self and the special gifts that you bring into the world.

1. What special qualities that were hidden before, can you now show from within yourself?

---

2. What were you telling the world about yourself in the past? Was this your old way of compensating for your negative belief, or were you hiding a deeper inner gift? How can you change this now?

---

3. What is it about you, that you now feel able to give to others and perhaps the world, based on your positive belief about yourself?

---

4. After you balance your beliefs your compensating skills are still there to be used, but now they are enhanced. They work as positive gifts since there is no need for them any longer to offset your unbalanced negative beliefs.
Example: Old negative belief *"I can't fix anything"*
New balancing Positive belief *"I like fixing things"*
My balanced compensating skills now tell me"
" I can help people fix their problems" .
What are some of your own examples *(Hint: think of your core issue word, in this example it would be "fix")*

---

5. What parts of your original authentic self, the person you were meant to be from the start, have until now, been missing, exiled or disowned?

---

6. What would you like to do now to help those parts begin to re-emerge and enhance your life?

Before Balancing

A common mistake, but understandable, is the idea that just getting rid of any kind of negative belief should make us feel better inside. People who try this find that somehow the positive effect, if any, does not last. There are good reasons for this.

1. A negative belief which formed in childhood fulfilled a very important purpose. It helped make sense of things or helped the child fit in a way that the child could accept (even though it was not true) "It is me who is not good enough because I ... . "

2. That's why the old negative belief became so deeply embedded. It's a bit like an old friend who has given tough but useful advice in the past when that was what was most needed. That same advice these days is neither accurate nor appropriate.

But you don't dump an old friend for that. However you must no longer follow their old advice. Instead you try to get them to upgrade their approach so they fit in with your life as it is now.

3. No matter what some psychotherapists tell you. You cannot actually "remove" a deeply embedded belief. You cannot unwire those old brain cells. But you can balance the old belief with a positive belief. That works.. Balancing is a natural process.

Before core beliefs are balanced

You're just so useless. No one could love you. *(Yes, that fits, that's me)*

You are just not good enough to succeed. Don't expect to win. *(Yes, that's, so true)*

What happened was all my fault. *(That fits, I deserve to get all t h e blame)*

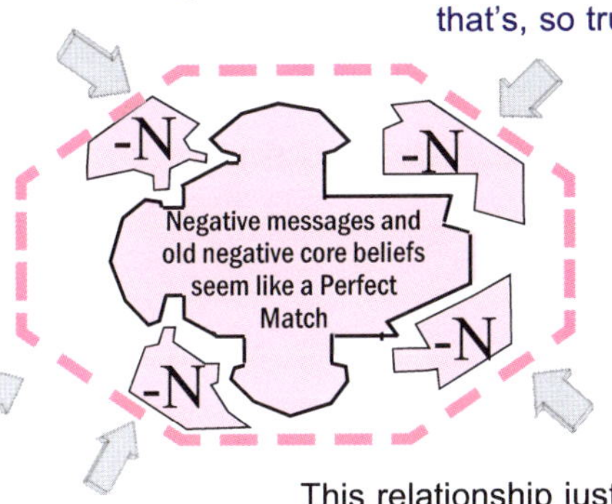

Give up - you are always wrong. *(Yes, that's me)*

This relationship just won't work. *(That fits, I always get it wrong.*
\

Seems like a "Perfect Match"

Before balancing your negative core beliefs, negative external events and negative messages about you seem as though they match perfectly, just like the pink negative **'- N'** messages in this diagram.

Bad experiences seem to match the way you see your vulnerability, they follow and support the negative views you hold about yourself. They appear to 'fit in' so neatly with the unbalanced but powerful views of your negative core belief.

Even though they are really not accurate or may even be totally false, you automatically accept them without question, you believe them. So then you set up repetitive "F" reaction patterns to try to deal with them. But the more your get stuck in those repeated "F" reaction patterns the more your negative core belief looks as if it is true. It seems like a "perfect match".

You are a person who really is worth loving. (No, I couldn't be! So what does he really want?)

What you are doing is working well. (That doesn't fit. I know it's not going to work much longer)

I deserve success. I'll keep working at it. *(Why bother? That will never fit for me.)*

Maybe this new relationship will work out for me? *(That doesn't fit. It will fail like all the other times)*

"No Deal?"

At the same time, before balancing, there does not seem to be any way that positive events or positive messages about you can fit in with the way your negative core belief sees you and the world around you.

Positive events appear to be in conflict with what your negative core beliefs tell you about yourself. Like the green positive **'P+'** symbols in the diagram above, those positive experiences will be rejected. ***No deal!***

You will find it very hard to accept or believe them because they just do not fit in with the picture of your personality which the negative core belief keeps telling you is the true "I am not good enough" you.

After core beliefs have been balanced

I am worthwhile and lovable just the way I am ***(That fits for me.)***

I'm often right. This could be one of those times. ***(That balances really for me.)***

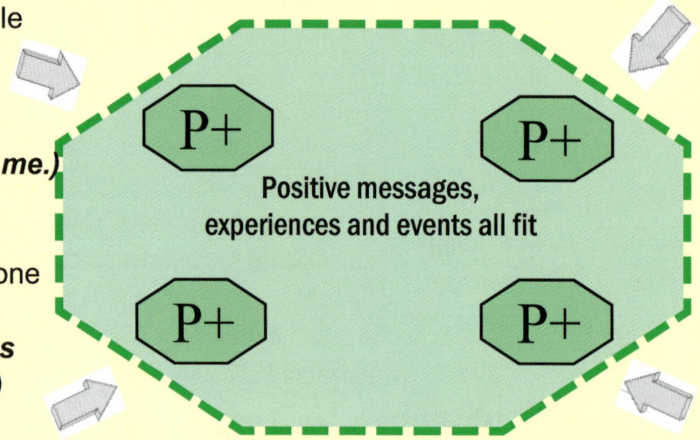

I like the way I did that. I got it right that time ***(That balances so well for me now.)***

As long as I don't rush it, I can enjoy this new relationship while I find out how it is going to work out. ***(That fits for me.)***

After balancing, positive messages about you, positive events and experiences all seem to fit in more easily with your balanced self image which is held in place by the self aware grown-up system inside you.

What it's like after balancing - an example

Once you stop being driven by the painful side of your core beliefs you begin to experience the positive nature of your real and natural self in relation to that same issue.

Example:

Originally stuck with a core belief:

I can't make things work

Old compensating skill:

Helping others make things work, but somehow I can't do the same for myself.

Positive balancing belief:

I can fix things that others cannot fix

Inner gift - my positive compensating skill and gift to others

My special gift is showing others better ways that they can use to fix things and make things work.

Other inner gifts, that would match opposite core beliefs:

I help people feel valued;

I understand people who need understanding;

I help people in pain to ease their pain;

I defend people who are being treated unfairly

If you complete Activity sheets CB-15 and CB-16 you will be able to identify your own unique and very special compensating skills, the ways they benefit you and the gifts they have brought you already.

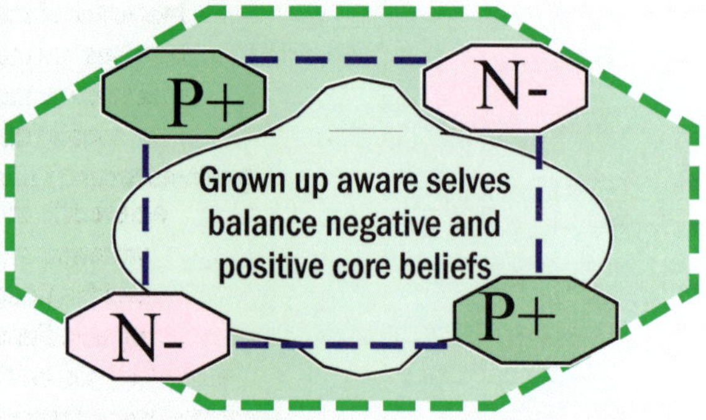

After balancing, events and information about you (both positive and negative) seem to fit much more easily with the self image held by the grown up aware selves. Even the most polarised inner selves are more easily held in balance as well.

How will I know when I have Balanced my two Beliefs?

There are many signs. People will treat you differently, in more positive ways. You will notice you have a more positive outlook about yourself and your future.

1. More and more of the things that you do or that people do with you seem to go right.
2. You no longer feel *"I am not good enough because I .... or I can't* or any of those other old feelings. Instead you experience a sense of having a weight lifted from your shoulders. You realise you now have enough resources (time, energy, skills, money, power, health, intellect, motivation, space, equipment etc.) to deal with most situations.
3. You are starting to expect that this is the way things should go in life. Your more grown-up more aware style, is becoming familiar.
4. You have far fewer F reactions, and those reactions will be under your control not automatic.
5. If you do occasionally feel vulnerable, defeated, overwhelmed or lost, this does not last for long.
6. You seldom feel that deep emotional pain inside even when you are triggered. It also does not last for long.
7. Certain words, actions or events may still 'trigger' your negative core belief but the result is much less severe. You don't often fly automatically into one of your old F patterns.
8. You notice quite quickly that when this happens, you can identify and name the reaction and then switch it off. You are no longer stuck with an automatic reaction. Now you have manual control of your reactions. Instead y**ou identify and name both your negative and positive belief**s (if it is safe to do so then out loud).
9. You can choose to change the way you react to old triggers and you find you are able to make the change without too much difficulty.
10. Sometimes you can tell in advance when a triggered reaction is about to happen. You discover you can switch it off just before it happens.
11. If you do get hooked back into one of your old "F" reaction patterns it is far less intense and uses up a lot less energy.
12. You no longer waste your time and other people's trying to get them to change the things they do or say to you, even if those things still upset you.
13. Less and less you find yourself making forecasts, predictions about how people are going to treat you and what you expect they will say to you, based on past repeated patterns.
14. You are glad that whatever you need to fix regarding your core belief problems is *"inside you"* and that you can balance your positive and negative core beliefs without needing help from someone else.
15. You understand that really there is nothing anyone else can do that will help make *your old belief* any better.
16. You are comfortable acknowledging and accepting the way that the old negative beliefs became a part of you a long time ago because in some way they were (at that time) needed to help you "fit in" as a member of your family or "make sense" of things that were going wrong around you as a child.
17. You accept and understand why your old belief can never be removed or "got rid of '. You remind yourself, how back then that belief was a kind of friend, a tough friend but that's what you needed to survive.

You understand why you don't kick old friends out because they are no longer needed or because their old job no longer exists. You also understand that you can instead update your old belief by giving it a positive role to play in the future by helping maintain balance.

18. You acknowledge other ways that having your old negative belief helped you, including the creation of the amazingly positive and useful "compensating skills" which you developed to help offset the negative belief.

These are truly a special "gift". After balancing they work even better for you.

Continued on next page

19. You understand how important it is to balance the negative belief with a positive core belief instead of trying to change the old belief or make it go away. Balancing the negative with a positive belief is the only way that works permanently.

No matter what some some psychotherapists may tell you, you understand why you cannot actually "remove" a deeply embedded belief. You cannot unwire those old brain cells. But you can balance the old belief with a positive belief.. That works. Balancing is a natural process.

20. You identify and name both your negative and positive beliefs (out loud with safe people but silently with others.

You understand that saying it this way does not make it stronger, as long as you identify it as 'my old unbalanced negative core belief' and add the words .. *"but today it is no longer true"*.

21. You keep noticing how in the past, in so many ways, the old belief controlled your daily life, choice of career and relationships.

One day you find yourself looking back and laughing about all this!

What today may seem a very serious matter loses its power.

You will no longer feel *"I am not good enough because I....* as you experience the reality of having the weight lifted from your shoulders.

You reconnect to your long lost sense of joy and exhilaration. Suddenly you find yourself laughing about that old unbalanced feeling even with friends and family.

It just isn't all that serious any more.. That is the day it has lost its power over you.

How you do this is explained in more detail in Books CBal-2 (Discovering Your Own Core Beliefs); and CBal-3 (Balancing your Core Beliefs)

See page 116 for details on how to get these two free books by e-mail.

Your aware grown-up systems help you take charge of your changes so you can:

* choose the best ways for you to change (how)
* choose the best time to make the changes (when)
* choose the best places to change (where)
* choose the best reasons for changing (why)
* choose only safe people to help you with your change (who)
* welcome these changes as a sign you are growing
* embrace your personal choices, options and opportunities as some of the most wonderful gifts life offers you every day.
* protect yourself from other people who want you to follow *their idea* of the how, when, where or why choices they think you should make.

Some Positive and well Balanced Core Beliefs

Positive beliefs or feelings about myself:	Life Issues
1. I am good enough (I feel safe; I can look after myself)	Security Safety
2. I am good enough (I belong; I don't feel too vulnerable)	Belonging, Nurture Self care
3. I am good enough (I have value, I am worthwhile)	Self worth
4. I am good enough (I have a sense of my personal power; Whatever I need, I can usually find)	Success Power Control
5. I am good enough (I am confident; I make sense)	Reality; Reason Knowing
6. I am good enough (My life is in balance)	Balance Moderation
7. I am good enough (I am me; I am who I am meant to be)	Identity; Recognition
8. I am good enough (I am aware and grown up and real)	Self awareness
9. I am good enough (I am lovable; I am included)	Love, Loved and Loving
10. I am good enough (I am healthy and whole)	Health; Self healing
11. I am good enough (I feel whole; connected with my inner spirit)	Wholeness; Spirit

The Universe will challenge your faith in each new belief

It always seems to do this

But it is not just 'something out there' trying to prove your old beliefs are still true

Most people experience a nasty jolt just after they achieve their first real experience of balancing their old belief with a new and positive one and they are feeling really optimistic about the future. It almost seems at that moment as if the universe deliberately sends them a couple of specially triggering experiences to restore the old negative belief.

See, it didn't work!

A client recently did some exceptionally powerful work with me balancing her negative belief *'I can't get it right'* and left in a very positive mood, but returned a minute later to say she had left the lights on in her car and the battery was flat. Her whole body language spelled out the message *'See, the balancing didn't work! I still can't get it right!'*

I had a similar experience with one of my own negative beliefs *'I am not valuable'*.

Working with gifted teacher Nikki Nemerof himself I finally saw mine (I have no value) clearly for the first time. But although it was a life changing experience for me I spent so long working through it with him that when I arrived at the lunch table I found there was no food left.

Immediately I told myself this was clear evidence the universe had singled me out as the only person in the group to miss out on lunch. That was all the 'proof' I needed to confirm that of all the people in the group I was *still* really the one person in the group who had no value.

It takes a little time to discover that lunches and flat batteries prove nothing in support of our old beliefs. It's part of the way our false beliefs work that gives us this impression.

The universe is challenging your faith, and only those with the strength of will to struggle against the old ways and the courage and grit to maintain their new belief continue to experience it

My friend got the car started in a couple of minutes and very soon I was rewarded with a specially made lunch which was better than anyone else's.

Most of the hundreds of people I work with report similar experiences about how easy it is, just after a completing a succesful balancing, to feel that the old belief has proved once again it still holds the power to control us.

This is not true. What these experiences do prove is that the spiritual side of us is working in the way it always does. The name you might know that side by (God, Jesus, Jehovah, Allah, Brahma, My Higher Power or any other name) makes no difference.

Expect to be tested

The most ancient spiritual writings from every great religious source, as well as so many ancient legends all tell us over and over again that when we take on a new belief, we can be expected to be tested in some way to help us determine the strength of our faith in that new belief.

As you find yourself experiencing events like these, remind yourself that this is a sign that your transformation process has already started.

The spiritual universe is challenging your faith, and encouraging you to hang on to your new strength, to struggle against the old ways and maintain your new positive belief as you continue to experience it each day.

Wanting others to feel your pain usually means you want them to fix it for you.

When you feel it by yourself, you can heal it by yourself

Your Six Key Self-aware Grown Up Life Skills

Your Life Issues

You already have these six Life skills. They were included in the package you got when you started life. But none of them work alone, each one interacts with all the others and each one helps all the other five. The better each skill is working today the better the others all work together and the better and more balanced you'll feel. Each one helps you function more effectively, with a more grown up sense of balance. Your key life skills help you deal with any of your vulnerability issues as they arise.

Your Identity and Self-esteem skills help you be more aware of how important it is to be who you really are; your history; your knowledge; your life experience. They remind you that things you do or did *are not part of who you are.*

These skills help you believe in yourself and your true self worth. Strong self esteem is when you can tell yourself *"I am worthwhile and valuable just as I am."; "I affirm my self value."* That makes it easier to hold a warm positive regard for others and to feel good about yourself when you give and receive compliments.

Your ability to set strong Boundaries

A boundary is an energetic shield which blocks negative energy coming at you from other people. Boundaries are a vitally important life skill helping protect you from feeling too vulnerable. They help you say 'no' or 'yes' to others in a healthy way.

Boundaries *help you set limits*, at the same time as you are being authentic in acknowledging you really are vulnerable. They help you understand and respect imperfections in others.

Boundaries help you develop a stronger sense of who you are and reject messages from other people when they try to tell you they know better than you who you are or try to get you to change yourself to be more the person they want you to be.

When people send you negative "You are..." messages it's your boundaries that remind you that *who you are is none of their business.*

Your Reality skills include your ability to hold a healthy sense of what is real for you, protecting it (your reality) from others who try to manipulate that part of you.

Key Life Skills or Life Issues that we can't live without

- Identity and Self-esteem
- Boundary setting and holding
- Reality and Noticing skills
- Balancing Self Nurturing and Loving
- Energy balancing, Moderation
- Security skills *(Safety, Sanity, Self)*

Reality skills help you to be more conscious of issues like truth; right-wrong; justice; fairness; openness and honesty; trust and trust-worthiness; your sense of reason and being reasonable. Together with your boundaries they help you avoid being manipulated.

Noticing

Your reality skills help you notice what is actually going on around you, compared with what may seem real to your young PYRO team. *(Some of them don't have very good eyesight.)*

Self-Nurturing Balanced with Loving others

You are able to take care of your own needs and wants appropriately. You come to understand that liking yourself is an essential part of healthy self nurturing, neither a fault nor vain, as some people would have you believe.

Self-nurturing also means you are able to reach out to others in a grown up way if you need to and ask for help to meet your needs and wants, and then accept the outcome *whether it is helpful for you or not.*

The better your self nurturing abilities the better you are at balancing complex issues like caring and sharing, keeping your giving and receiving in balance. You can balance unconditional loving with conditional commitment; exploring the many different ways you can choose to give and receive love and nurturing.

Energy Balancing skills help you sit comfortably between opposites in your life, to ***moderate*** any polarised or extreme (too black or too white) patterns in the way you think, speak or act.

Options, opportunities and alternatives

Balancing skills open up your ability to see options, opportunities and alternatives that enrich your life. There are almost always more than two possible ways of dealing with life's problems. It's not just black and white.

Security skills (Safety, Sanity, Strength,Self, Spirit) help you stay aware of your vulnerability; your ability to protect your self and maintain your safety, sanity, strength, self and spirit too.

The law of energetic balance that rules our lives

Polarised energies

For each energy state or inner self within you there exists an opposite energy or an opposite self. Often both are inside you. Many times the opposite one is outside of you. You cannot get rid of either one of them and if you try to, that one will find other ways to come back to you to try to maintain your energetic balance.

For example, if one side within you, such as positive thoughts and feelings, gets too strong then, somewhere outside of you, (or inside you) the opposite negative energy will build up in some way to try to maintain the balance.

This has a significant effect on the way you react towards other people, with the energies in them when they are with you and so how each of you interacts with the other.

As you become more aware of strength of the law you also realise that it is your aware grown up system alone that has the ability to create a real balance between opposite energies. Each time you become aware of a particular energy that is polarised (either too strong or too weak) in you, you understand more about things that seem to 'go wrong' around you and discover new ways to fix them.

Balancing creates positive energy

- Balancing the 'best parts' (the positive energies) between other people and yourself creates more positive energy in both people and maintains the positive balance.
- The more positive energy you send towards another person the more you empower them to grow in positive ways and to make their own changes the way they need to.

Opposite Energies can be only be balanced. Neither one can be switched on or off

For thousands of years, people have recognised that although energies may seem separate and opposite, they are really a duality and that together they create one whole. Different cultures just chose different names. One of the very earliest was Yin and Yang.

Opposite Energies can only be balanced, not switched on or off

After reading this, you might however decide to skip balancing and instead cease immediately your old habit of criticising your partner and instead apply lots of positive energy towards him or her in the hope of gaining better balance. Wrong.

If you attempt this too rapidly, that means your younger protector parts are doing a fast flip rather than letting your aware grown up system create the balance. Opposite Energies can be balanced, they cannot be switched on or off.

Changing energy levels too rapidly like this, or attempting to switch them on or off can cause others around you unconsciously to make equally rapid changes *to maintain the previous imbalance* and also to reduce the vulnerability of too rapid change.

In the example above, your partner who was normally happy and positive (to balance your previous negative energy) may suddenly become destabilised, sad, angry or even get sick. Balancing energies through your aware grown up system avoids this.

Unbalanced negative energy

- Most of the negative things that happen around you contain valuable lessons you need to learn. Whether it seems like it at the time or not, something good usually comes out of something bad.

Negative events often have a way of turning out, unexpectedly, for the best. When one door closes another door opens.

- Sending negative energy towards another person increases negative or disempowering energy in both of you.
- If any of your inner selves act from the false position that what *they do* will stop or change something *another person' selves are doing,* the harder that person's selves will fight back.

The more your inner selves apply negative energy (attacking, judging, criticising, arguing, pressuring, punishing, shaming, blaming) towards other people's inner selves the stronger the other person's selves resistance.

The positive change you hoped for is less likely.

For many people, myself included, too much polarised energy applied towards mechanical and electronic objects seems to produce a similar result.

Corollaries

- The more you understand your own vulnerability or pain, the more you can understand and guide others facing the same issues
- If you feel fear inside you will find fear outside you
- Only after you can rely on yourself can you start to rely on others
- Unless you feel safe alone with yourself you will not feel safe with other people.
- If you care too much for other people you will not care enough for yourself
- Until you really love yourself you cannot really love anyone else
- If you trust your own judgement (reality) you will be comfortable with others who have a different reality of their own
- The more you can be who you really are the more others can be themselves with you
- If you find it hard to accept compliments you'll find it hard to give them
- To the degree that you can enjoy your own company *alone* you will attract people as friends who are equally comfortable with themselves. If you are uncomfortable with yourself, that's the kind of people you will attract
- The better your own boundaries the less trouble you will have with other people whose boundaries are not working
- When parents use too much negative energy to stamp out a particular way of thinking, feeling or acting in their family (for example spontaneity, rebellion or sexual energy) that pattern is likely to become dominant in *one or more* of their children.

Typical polar opposite energy states

Each one of your primary or active and visible protector characters has an energetic opposite. One may be highly visible, the other in the background or it may be well hidden. Often they are out of balance. Your opposites are also usually different to the ones in people you know.

- positive and negative energies
- primary or very strong and disowned or very weak energies
- personal and impersonal energies
- doing and being energies
- thinking and feeling energies
- younger fighter of fixer and younger more vulnerable peacekeeper energies
- empowered and disempowered
- predictable and unpredictable
- successful and unsuccessful or failure
- can't do it and 'give it a go' energies
- peace keeper (pleaser) and open honest and blunt
- difficult and easy
- long and short
- high and low
- integrity and manipulative or rip-off

Your examples:

_ _

_ _

_ _

_ _

Why Core Belief Balancing works

Anyone who has made even a brief connection with their inner selves (inner voices) knows how positive and easy it is to use the technique called 'voice dialogue'. It is so natural in fact, that most people find themselves talking with some of their more accessible inner selves within minutes of starting a session.

Having these casual two-way conversations with your own inner selves, is natural, positive and very helpful, particularly when you get to talk with a pair of inner selves who are each trying to help you but are locked in conflict over what you should or should not do about life's problems (take that new job, don't take it; work harder, take it easy; fight, give in; leave him now, stay on and try to fix things).

Typical inner selves have a strong desire to be recognised. They are keen to tell us about what they are doing to protect our vulnerability, what they want us to do to make life easier or how they each think we should act to fix things.

Most inner selves welcome an opportunity to have a conversation or dialogue, so the process is quite easy.

All it needs to encourage one or more of the selves to start talking is an interviewer, who plays a non-judgemental role.

It takes only a little practice and does not require special skill or training.

Talking with two opposite inner selves gives you the awareness you need to separate each of them from the other.

Balance works better

This helps bring balance back into your life, and works far more effectively than trying to get rid of either of them.

Neither you nor a counsellor or therapist can remove an inner self

The brain cells are hard wired and have powerful restoration systems to keep them in place no matter what you try.

Honouring and Embracing

This understanding is at the heart of Voice dialogue. The more you honour and express appreciation during your conversations with an inner self the more you learns about them.

If you listen they will guide you with vital clues.

Core Belief work is NOT Therapy. It cannot 'heal' nor 'cure' nor 'fix'

Self awareness and self empowerment training is a powerful process. But it is NOT therapy and must never be presented as if it was therapeutic in nature.

It is in no way suggested as a cure or treatment for any diagnosable condition, whether physical or psychological in nature.

It may however compliment other treatments by helping you develop a more positive outlook about yourself, your body, your self-esteem and your authentic vulnerability. If a diagnosable condition is partly or largely related to non-physical or ACE issues the chances of improvement are then likely to increase.

Balance your Life with Emotional Gym

Faster Relief Less Stress

Balancing your Personal power with Emotional Gym is a gentle but dynamic process that has proved to grow self-empowerment, resolve underlying stresses, release blockages, barriers and deep body memories and helps you create powerful changes in your life, with more joy and less pain.

It's a dynamic *body movement process* that incorporates the growing understanding that so many of life's issues are stored even more in our bodies than in our brains, as shown in studies of Adverse Childhood Experiences (ACE) and Polyvagal Theory but I prefer to work with all that without those psychological explanations.

Best of all Emotional Gym is a safe do-it-yourself process.

Emotional Gym - Aims

To tie together some of the latest and powerful understandings about stress, fear, vulnerability and body pain including:

1. How and why so many of life's big problems are stored in your body as well as your head.
2. Why tuning in to those body messages is often the beginning of resolving those big issues.
3. Sharing with you some straight forward, safe and easy do-it-yourself ways to work with those painful or scary body sensations without going into deep psychological explanations.

These are Positive Processes

Core Belief Balancing and Emotional gym are very positive processes. As you work on each step you will experience positive outcomes and plenty of improvements that are waiting for you in your life, your work, your relationships and your joy of living.

This is a do-it-yourself process

This book will guide you but in the end it is about a tool kit that you hold in your own hands and can use for the rest of your life to enhance your self empowerment and love of being alive.

Acknowledgement

I need to make it clear that I don't claim to have come up with the idea of emotional gym. I'm not sure if I even originated the term "Emotional Gym" but I have added a few features as I discovered how powerful emotional gym was and how easily people found it working for them as a way to *reduce stress and feelings of vulnerability and restore a sense of balance in their life.*

However I acknowledge that the originators of emotional balancing are two amazing psychologists in the USA, Dr. Hal Stone and Dr, Sidra Stone who developed the Psychology of the Aware Ego and the process of Voice Dialogue. I trained with them for several years during the 1990s. I also acknowledge Dr. Martha Lou Woolf who today continues to train the world in their work. I continue to learn from her as we work on Skype.

That's Emotional Gym. It's Safe and fast and it works.

4. Why embracing and then balancing two opposite body energies works far better than trying to limit either one or the other of them (which cannot work)
5. The close connection with your ever changing emotional age and everything else that is going on inside and outside you including stress, fear, pain.
6. The false belief that power is mostly outside of you. An unbalanced and too young emotional age pattern is what locks this false belief in.
7. Looking at your Adverse Childhood Experiences (ACE) and the effects on your life of even a moderate ACE score
8. Discovering your old core beliefs and their effects on your life and balancing those too.
9. Balancing your sense of vulnerability and not enough vulnerability
10. Balancing Self empowerment vs disempowerment.

Setting up for Emotional Gym

Set up three, four or more chairs in a row or a sit on a three or four seat sofa. You can even do emotional gym sitting on the side of your bed as long as you're clear on where the "middle" position is.

It's so easy

For a start sit first in this centre chair / position and get ready to move in turn into both the left and the right side chairs.

The middle position is the "safe" position

This is also described as your "safe" chair. If you ever find that sitting in another chair is distressing move straight back to the middle and feel the safety.

Now you're the middle but get ready to move to one of the side chairs, it doesn't matter which one.

Stop thinking about which side or why!

Try not to think about which chair, which side or "why" you are going to chose any chair. There is no significance in your choice but too much thinking, analysing logically or looking for a "why" before you move will slow or even block the gym process.

If there is any authentic reason why you chose a particular chair it will become clearer after you complete the gym.

When you are ready, just move and the faster the better!

Dynamic Emotional Gym

First move

Emotional Gym is a dynamic process. You use your body as well as your mind. You exercise both together. So let's make things more active.

From the middle chair, quite quickly move physically over to one of the chairs on the left or right (it doesn't matter which one). You may prefer to stand or sit on the floor.

While you are over there on that side, try to identify that position as the physical location of one specific part of your energy or inner protector system. Try to identify that place as a one part of you, one of your protector parts or one of your sub-personalities.

You have moved. How do you feel sitting there? What do you think about?

There are some useful questions you might ask yourself as you sit there. See point 4 below

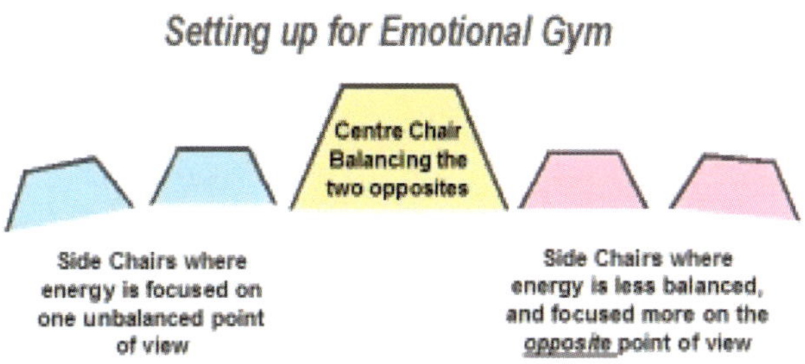

Second move Back to the Middle

After a minute or less sitting that side return to the centre chair.

Try to develop a sense that as you move back to the middle chair you are separating from the energy in that side chair. Imagine it's still over there in its side chair waiting for its turn to be recognised again.

Each time you sit in the middle chair you're getting a dynamic sense of what it's like here, sitting in your more balanced and more grown up part of you.

Growing that feeling is one of the primary aims of Emotional Gym.

The other aim is to give you a sense of how natural it is to have opposite energies, in fact it's normal and it is so easy to balance those opposite energies instead of fighting them.

However at the start you might notice your stress levels rising. That will soon settle down.

Third move

Now move to the opposite side chair. See if it feels like that position is connecting you to a different kind of energy in your body. This may not happen the first or second time. Keep going. It will happen.

The more you can feel some sense of an opposite point of view the better. Let it out. You need those two opposites to do the most important part of emotional gym, the balancing of the two opposites.

Fourth move

When you feel ready, move back to the middle chair. You might now sense why this is like working in a gym, it's quite a physical process and you're working more with your body than your mind.

NOTE: You do need to move physically at least one full body width away from each previous position. Sitting in any one spot and thinking about moving without moving your body won't work

Fifth move

Return again to the first opposite chair or position. Feel yourself returning to that same energy that was there before. Stay there for ten or twenty seconds or longer.

Keep repeating the Five Emotional Gym steps

Keep going backwards and forwards but always going to the middle chair between each side move.

Repeat the same moves ten or twenty of more times, just as you would in a gym.

As you sit in each of the three chairs or positions including the middle, feel yourself returning to that same energy that was there before. Stay there for ten or twenty seconds maybe more.

Pause a little longer every so often in the middle

Notice, as you sit in the middle how your stress levels are lowering. You are feeling less vulnerable. That's because your emotional strength is developing, your sense of being in a grown up state of self awareness is also growing stronger.

Getting ready to work on your Emotional Balancing

Notice, as well as you sit in the middle that as your stress levels get lower, your sense of emotional balance is improving. There are many different ways of developing this.

Questions you in the middle position might ask the parts on each side:

1. When you are over on the left hand side / chair can you feel the source of your energy located in a specific place in your body? Where is that place?

2. When you are over on the left hand side / chair what emotional age do you feel you are?

3. When you're over on the right hand side / chair can you feel the source of your energy located in a specific place in your body? Where is that place?

4. When you're over on the right hand side / chair what emotional age do you feel you are?

5. Dynamic Emotional Balancing

At this point you are ready to start adjusting the energy levels on either side.

For a start you may notice that one side is much stronger than the other one.

Just moving backwards and forward will help but often it's not enough.

Imagine a see-saw (sometimes called a teeter-totter) A long board with seats at each end and balanced on a central point so you can move each end up and down

Imagine that the part of your team that has been sitting on the left is a heavyweight while the one on the right is smaller and not as strong. That means their energies are out of balance and if you look at the way they feel when you are over on each of "their" sides you'll see how this imbalance is affecting your life, your work, your finances, your relationships and even your health.

Adjusting their weights to get a better balance is the next step. And your emotional gym is just the right place to work on a weight loss program for the heavyweight part while the weaker part starts working on some body building exercises

A safe and a very easy process - and it's not therapy

I have used this process with clients and trainees for more than 20 years. It has different names but it's best known by the term, "Voice Dialogue". But this safe, magical and powerful process has a lot more to do with emotional age and inner child work than with voices.

It was developed and is still being developed by two incredible psychologists in the United States Dr. Hal Stone and Dr. Sidra Stone.

Emotional gymnasium work closely follows their basic voice dialogue set-up.

Hal and Sidra Stone stress that this is not therapy because first it is *not intended to treat, fix or heal any diagnosable condition* and should never be used with that intention. It is only a way of helping a person become more self aware and increase their sense of self empowerment.

A counsellor or facilitator is only supporting a client while he or she is doing the gym. The client is always in charge of their process.

You can find out lots more about this process if you go to my website: *http://www.realme1.com/EGym42.html*

Activity Sheet R -2 Date __/__/__

Practice being your Grown up Self Aware Real Me - Emotional Gym

A powerful do-it-yourself process to grow your Self Awareness

Find a safe and preferably a quiet place where you can move freely to the left or to the right of a central position. A long couch or the side of a bed is OK. Three or more separate chairs work best.

1. Choose which you would like to be the middle chair or place. This is where you sit (or stand) each time you move *intentionally* into your real grown up self aware real me. Also described as the *'safe chair.'*

2. Sit in that centre position, relax. Feel the safety here.

3. Choose an issue or problem you are dealing with in your life *at present*, something where there are two or more sides, two or more choices and each side has plus and minus features.

4. Imagine you are now sitting between your two opposite selves or energetic states. Though opposite in their outlook, be aware they are actually paired. But do not imagine that either your left or right will automatically be the positive or negative, weak or strong side. *Do not label either side as good or bad.*

5. When you feel drawn to ***one*** of the side chairs or positions on the couch, then consciously move ***your whole body*** to that position. Imagine you are leaving your self aware grown up side remaining in the centre and will be returning.

6. In your chosen new position you are now free to take one side only on the opposite issues. While there, you can, if you like, be quite strongly biased about 'your' point of view, even critical of 'your' opposite.

7. Notice the energy in your body as you sit in that point of view. How strong is it? Often you'll notice it's focussed in a point somewhere in your body. What emotional age do you feel are? If it's a doing energy identify ***what*** that side does to protect all of you. However, try <u>not to think about 'why</u>.' Instead think abo*r* *what colour fits best* for you here. Move or angle your chair towards or away from the middle to match your feelings. When doing Voice Dialogue your facilitator can ask each part these questions, but it's quite safe and easy to do this by yourself.

8. If you feel too scared or too vulnerable when you sit in a chair don't stay there. Move back quickly to the safety of the middle chair. Start again with another different topic.

9. If the side you are sitting in is comfortable that you have experienced it's point of view, return to the middle chair, sensing that as you do this you are going back to being your real grown up again and leaving that energy in its side chair.

10. Now do the same with the other side repeating steps 5 to 9 the same way. Then go back to the centre again. Notice how you are feeling when you return to the middle.

11. If you feel like continuing, repeat the whole process, with a different opposite pair. Or repeat the gym with the same two inner selves. Both sides will still be in their chairs waiting for you.

Here are some examples of paired opposites.
There are hundreds of others like these

Don't imagine that either left or right will automatically be the position for positive or negative, weak or strong. If you feel like talking, or writing while in any particular chair this is particularly valuable, so let it happen in what ever way feels most comfortable.

Six areas of Vulnerability

All living things feel vulnerable. It's a natural state. As humans we are very conscious of our vulnerability levels as they constantly change from, let's say 1 to 100. We need to be aware of this or we would take too may risks. But nobody gets to feel a vulnerability level of less than one.

From the start of childhood we are constantly looking for ways to reduce our vulnerability and our feelings or fear about feeling vulnerable.

There are at least six areas where every person is Vulnerable

1. Survival and Safety - events that scare you or increase your fear, especially real danger

2. Strength - events that lower your power to deal with your stress and vulnerability

3. Sanity - experiences that cause you to doubt your reality or your natural common sense.

4. Self - experiences that rob you or steer you away from your right to be authentic, the person you really are.

5. ***Success*** - events or experiences that slow, delay, block or disempower you, so you can't make the changes you want to make in your life.

6. Spirit - experiences that weaken your spirit the powerful force within you to grow, to enjoy life and share your gifts with others.

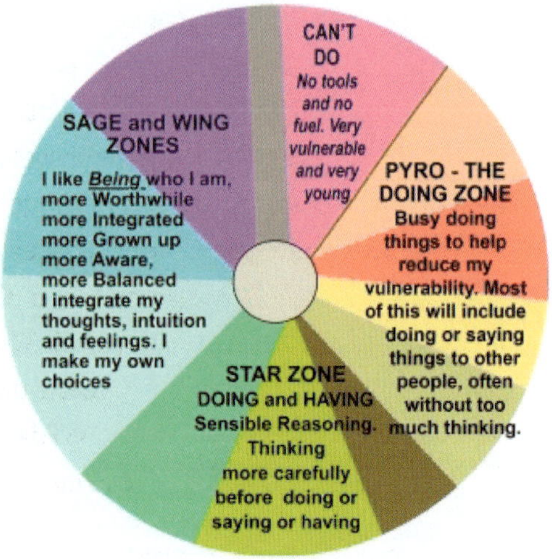

ACE s - Adverse Childhood Experiences

An adverse childhood experience is an event or a series of events that causes us to feel scared, fearful, stressed or more vulnerable, or when we're hurt physically and emotionally or both.

I recommend talking about ACE rather than using terms like "trauma" and "abuse." Sure, those words describe some of the most serious childhood events but any experiences that had a strong effect on you in childhood, regardless of what we call them carry over into adulthood.

Scientists and skilled health professionals are now discovering that the higher your total ACE score the more problems you can expect in your life, effects on physical health, body pain, financial problems, relationship break-downs, career issues, high stress, addictions, blockages, boundaries, psychological dis-orders and more.

These are symptoms rather than the real problems. You may just be in the grip of a high ACE score.

Resolving ACE based issues even pain in your body is much easier than treating a medically defined problem This also avoids prescription drugs which do not help resolve ACE issues anyway.

Identifying the original cause is a major step forward in dealing with each of those problems, the result of early childhood trauma and a very high ACE score.

My experimental ACE survey is available free as a pdf file, sent by e-mail

Just e-mail me

bligh4@growingaware.com

... and I'll send you my latest ACE survey so you can calculate your own ACE score.

(It's free of course)

Or download it from my website

www.ACE.realme1.com

Using your Emotional Age Wheel with Core Belief Balancing

***EA is** your skill*

***Your coloured EA wheel is** your tool kit*

Emotional Age Awareness (EA) is a powerful life skill. The better you are at EA the more powerful you are and the more successful your life.It adds essential understanding about everything you think and do and say and feel.

Your emotional age patterns keep changing each day and usually each hour as things change around you. There is no such thing as a fixed emotional age.

Traditionally, people talk about three emotional styles, parent, child and adult. That's not accurate because the way so your called 'parent' parts behave shows they are actually still very young emotionally. They're just pretending to be grown up, trying to sound judgemental or bossy like a parent, as their way of trying to protect you. It doesn't work very well.

The EA coloured wheel is a clearer picture of what's really going on. It identifies your different emotional age patterns as they ocurr during the day using colour and four code words to keep it simple.

Four EA groups WING, STAR, PYRO and SAGE

Let's start with the PYRO ones, who developed in childhood as your first inner protector patterns when there was nothing else to protect you. They remain forever young, emotionally. PYRO summarises some of the things these younger parts do. They are:

Protecting you *but in their particular style*

Young emotionally *but*

Ready to act *instantly* and

Over-active There are so many examples:

**over-defensive; over-protective; over-reacting; over-responsible; too extreme; trying too hard; over-explaining; over-justifying; overly critical; overly judgemental; too busy blaming; trying too hard to please other people; talking too much; telling too much;*

Young PYRO selves don't do things by halves.

Many of these over active PYRO patterns include rapidly switching backwards and forwards between two polarised opposites: It's either all black or all white.

Your emotional age patterns keep changing each day and usually each hour as things change around you. There is no such thing as a fixed emotional age.

Reactions are polarised, with no options in between the two extremes, no chance of a flexible balance. Examples: *Too fast or too slow; too black or too white; too quiet or too loud; too brave or too scared; sometimes stuck; sometimes switching positions too quickly, hoping for a fast fix; full steam ahead or full stop.*

Note: As a general observation, the more extreme, the further apart two polarised opposite positions appear to be, the more likely that they are linked to a history of too many childhood ACEs.

Flipping - a sudden PYRO shift between opposites

Typically there will be a sudden shift, a flip, between polar opposite positions. Reactions switch too quickly or swing backwards and forwards between too far apart opposite positions, jumping from A to Z with no pause in between and without thinking it through first.

Some PYRO go out and battle the world like brave little soldiers, others fight like rebel teenagers. Some play the 'pretend parent' role. Some just pressure themselves (and you too) to work harder and harder.

A 'young' (in EA terms) inner self's view of the world is not always reliable.

Is it's focus too much on doing? Is it too intense as it over-explains its reasons for what it's doing? Is it trying too hard to be logical. That's a young or very young emotional self trying too hard.

However, if during a dialogue, it describes what it is *being* or *not being* that's more reliable.

However, if during a dialogue, it describes what it is *being* or *not being* that's more reliable.

STAR and WING

Your STAR patterns are more logical so they may be a bit short on feelings and empathy but they do a better job protecting you than your PYRO team, because they are more grown up emotionally.

WING patterns are mature, flexible and more authentic and even more grown up. They provide the best protection.

PYRO still want their old jobs back

Most PYRO selves are also stuck with an attitude that today there still isn't anyone else on your team who knows how to protect you as well as they do. They were there first, when there was nobody else and have stayed on the job all your life, how could newcomers like STAR and WING hope to do as well?

The PYRO team still believe you can't rely on those newer parts like WING, or STAR. Yes, maybe when things are going smoothly but if they get really difficult for you, some of the young PYRO will take over automatically like a sprinkler system with the first sign of smoke. They won't check first.

The 'O' in PYRO stands for "Over active" but an alternate attitiude for the 'O' in PYRO could be "Only I can fix this!"

Let your grown up parts drive

EA gives you the ability to see this happening and consciously connect to your more real, more powerful energy patterns, your grown up parts who these days are really better equipped to protect all of you and specially your most vulnerable part, the PINK on the EA wheel.

If other people are trying to control or manipulate you, EA helps you strengthen the parts of you that stop that happening. EA also helps you understand what drives other people to think and feel and do and say things such as manipulating or undermining you.

> Your emotional Age is not fixed and it is not a number. It is a highly energised force moving inside you.
>
> As it changes, it can drive you from feeling like a confident grown up to a vulnerable child in one second, from senior citizen to excited teenager the next minute then back again. It has absolutely no connection with your age according to the clock or calendar.

Tune in to other people's EA as well

We may see ourselves as 'civilised' but underneath are parts of us still ruled by instinct, intuition and similar energies.

Like all creatures, we still tune in to the energies in people around us and react accordingly, partly out of reason or logic but often more in an instinctual way guided by the energies projected by the inner selves (one of ours and one of theirs) who are trying to handle the situation.

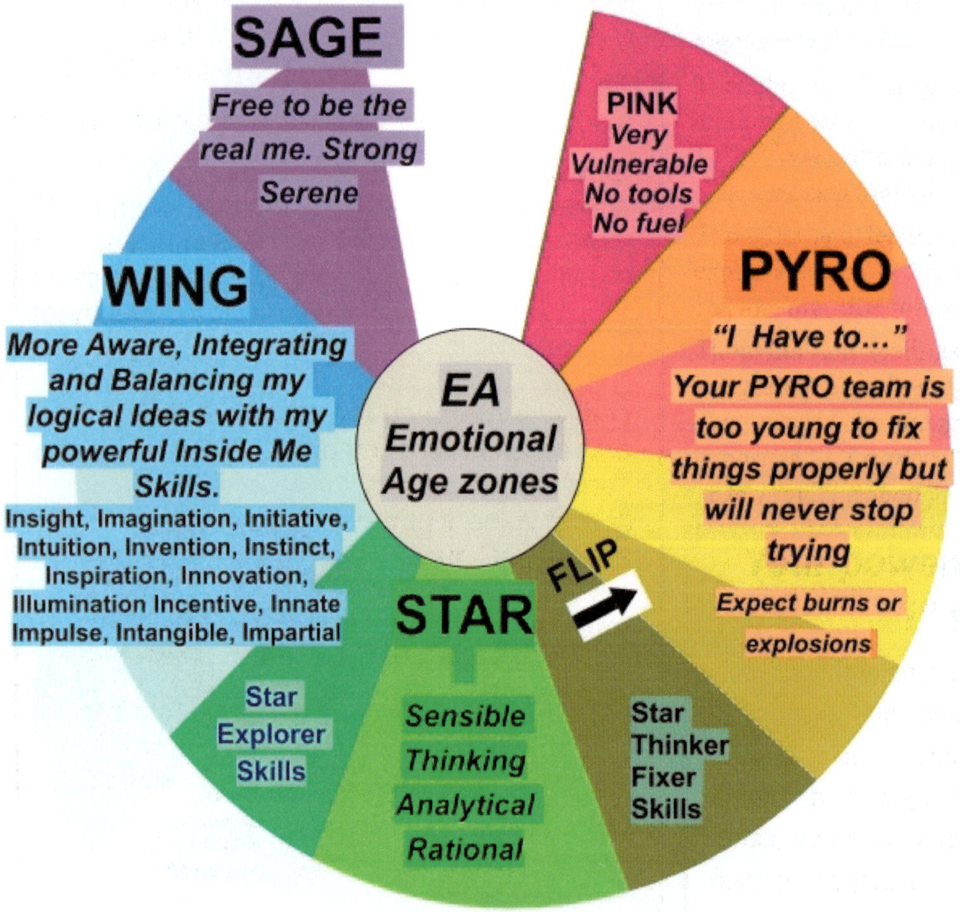

Your emotions and the way you deal with negative events in life will change each day or each hour as your Emotional Age changes to fit each situation. Nobody has just one fixed emotional age all the time.

Look at your <u>intensity</u> level and what that intensity is focussed on. Is it doing, thinking, choosing or being.

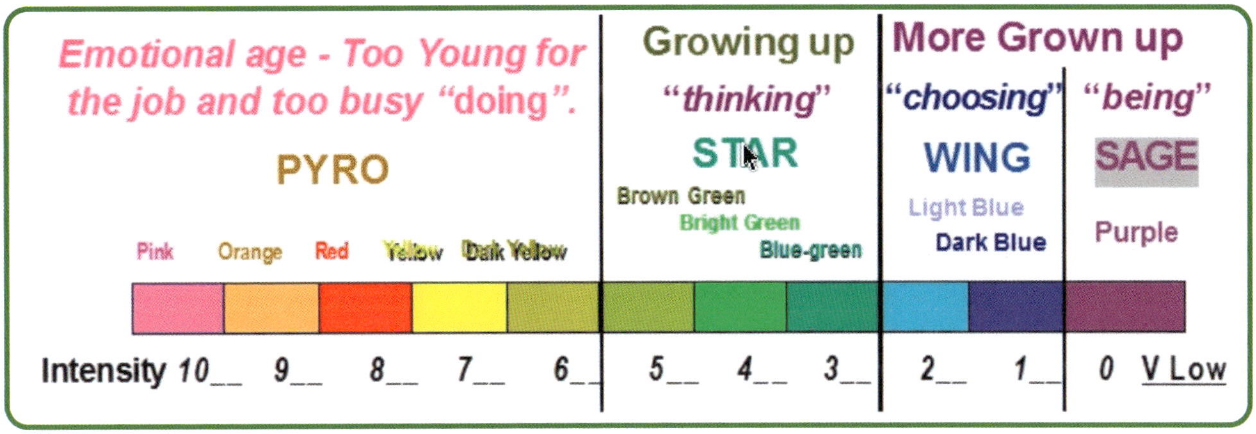

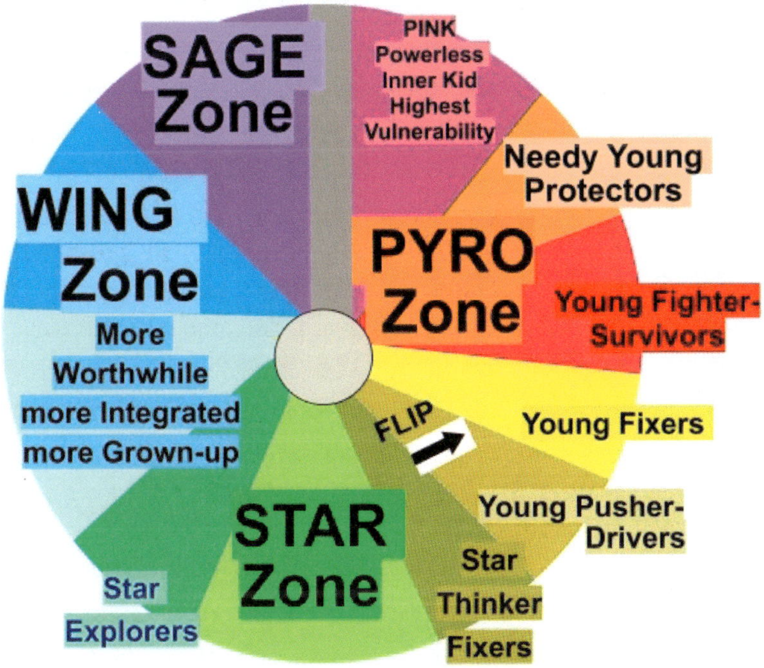

Your Emotional Age awareness helps you understand your most troublesome F reactions

EA helps you to see how most F over-reactions are driven by emotions that developed in childhood or early teens.

Words that tell you if one of your own particular inner selves (or another person's)is taking a grown-up approach, or if it's a young inner self 'driving your bus' at that particular moment.

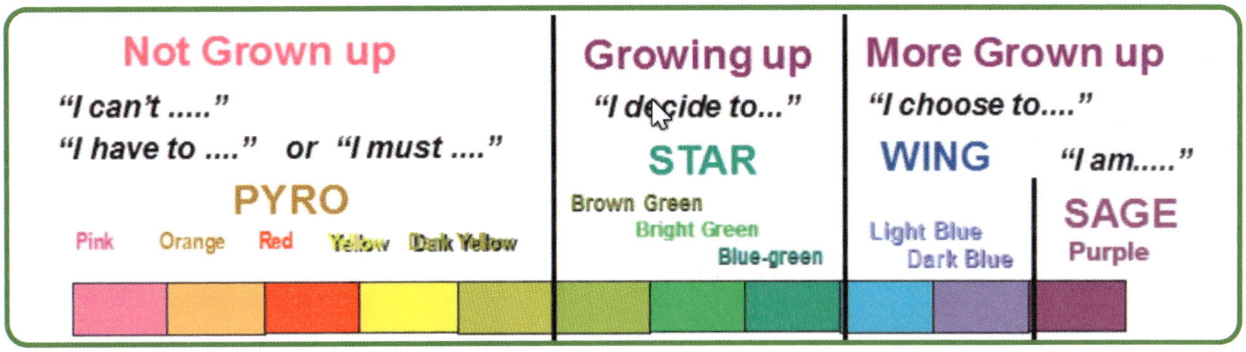

Your Four EA zones

PYRO Colours: Pink Orange Red Yellow and Dark Yellow

PYRO - when you're in this EA zone you're trying hard but often not succeeding in managing your life using skills that you learned a long time ago. Your emotional age at these times is young or very young. Young protector members of your PYRO team include young peacekeepers, young fighter-survivor-rebels, young fixers and young pusher-drivers.

Leaving your younger PYRO team free to drive your emotional bus can cause lots of clashes, and collisions, while they collect emotional speeding tickets, start emotional fires or explosions and may occasionally lead to episodes where they encourage you to shoot yourself in the foot.

STAR Colours: Brown Green, Bright Green and Blue-green

STAR - When you move to this EA zone you'll be more sensible more rational than any of your young protectors can be. You'll find you are better at thinking and growing and standing firm.

WING Colours: Light Blue and Dark Blue

WING - When you move to this EA zone your life is much more positive and quite different. You feel more worthwhile, more integrated, more grown up, more balanced more aware more joy.

Colour: Purple

SAGE Self Aware Grown up Energy - When you are in this EA zone you really can be who you are, the real "me". You'll enjoy feeling your Self Aware Grown up "I am who I am" energy.

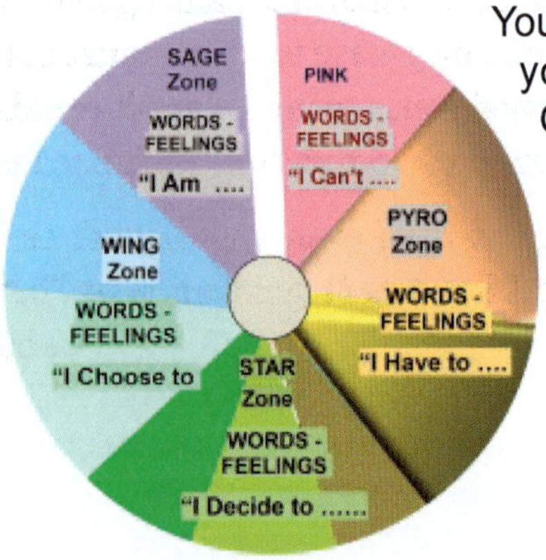

Words, Thoughts and feelings

Typical thoughts and feelings in the pink very young very vulnerable sector - *"I should .... but I can't; I wish .....", I just can't cope any longer, I feel like giving up. It's all too much." "I just can't work it out". "I just can't go on" "I am lost". "I give up". "I shouldn't have to do this". "I'm frightened".*

Typical thoughts and feelings in the orange young and needy sector - *"I have to .... , I ought to ....."* and *"You have to .... , You ought to ....." "I need you to fix it."*

Typical thoughts and feelings in the red young fighter-survivor-rebel sector are *"I must .... or you must ....(action)····"*

Typical thoughts in the bright yellow young fixer sector - *"It needs fixing."; "Either I will fix it or you will fix it ....";*

Typical thoughts in the dark yellow young pusher-driver sector - *"One way or the other let's just get it fixed ...." "Let me tell you how to fix it."*

Thoughts in the green-brown thinking fixer sector are *"What can we do to fix it?"; "How can we work together to fix it?"*

Thoughts and feelings in the green STAR sensible thinking sector - *"I decide to; I think first and then I .."; "I can look at things sensibly."; "I can see when I am not being logical."*

Thoughts and feelings in the blue green STAR explorer sector *"I need to think about that."; " I can explore, discover new ways to fix things ....";*

Thoughts and feelings in the blue more aware imagining plus feeling WING sector - *"I can choose and I can change ....."; "I can balance my opposites." "I explore"; "I have these options."; "I feel joy."; empathy;*

Your powerful Inside Me "I" skills

Use Your Imagination, Initiative, Intuition, Empathy, Innovation, Inspiration, Illumination, Innate-understanding, Inventing, Intangible thoughts, Impartial Ideas, Incentive, Impulse, Instinct, and of course Integration.

Talk to the Author, John Bligh Nutting on Skype or preferably Zoom It's free

If you've come this far I am sure you now understand a lot more about your core beliefs. Congratulations.

I have been sharing my books like this one with people around the world for nearly 20 years. Each week I receive e-mail and calls from readers who describe how my work has helped them make powerful and positive changes in their lives.

I also get e-mails asking questions, discussing what they have discovered, wanting to know more. In the past I replied by email but today with Zoom and Skype talking face to face has proved so much more effective. Typing those answers took too much time.

With Zoom Professional or Skype you can ask questions and get an immediate answer. With our web cameras on it's almost the same as talking face to face. Even serious discussions and a modified EMDR are now as easy as if we were in the same room.

You don't need to install Zoom on you computer. It runs via the Cloud.

> *Time Differences - I am in Brisbane Queensland Australia*
>
> ***(we do not have daylight saving in this State)***
>
> Middle East - I am 7 hours ahead of you
>
> Europe - I am 8 hours ahead of you
>
> East Coast USA - I am 12-13 hours ahead of you
>
> West Coast USA - I am 17 hours (one day minus 7 hours} ahead of you. Example: When it is 8:00 pm Monday in California it is 1:00 pm Tuesday in Brisbane
>
> Use this link to find out the best time to connect.
>
> **http://www.timeanddate.com/worldclock/meeting.html**
>
> Once I have confirmed the day and time you can be confident we will be talking soon afterwards.

I already enjoy talking with readers in the United States, Canada, United Kingdom, Germany, France, Italy, Africa, the Pacific and a number of Middle East and South-East Asian countries.

This is my invitation to you to join me if you have questions and you would like a direct answer. You can start setting up our contact now. However I cannot talk with you on unless we have arranged the day and time in advance.

* We need to set a day and a time because Zoom isn't like Skype. You can't call like you can on a phone
* Because we are on the other side of the world, morning where you are could be after midnight here, or the other way round.

However, once we have booked the day and time you can be confident we will be talking soon afterwards.

What does this cost?

A short Skype, Zoom or phone question-and-answer talk or a brief discussion for ten or twenty minutes is free to anyone who has already purchased any of my Growing Awareness or Flying Awareness books, including this copy.

E-mail me please and make a time.

John Nutting is my name

bligh4@growingaware.com

> **With Skype and Zoom I am now able to work with you when you are using the highly successful EMDR (Eye Movement Desensitising and Reprocessing) system . There's a free EMDR app for your iPhone or Android unit.**

Are you are reading this book on Kindle?

I am hoping you will choose to take the next step in resolving your Unbalanced Core Belief issues and then balancing them with your positive core beliefs. Here's what you do next.

These books are free. All you need to do is ask

There are two more do-it-yourself books that follow this book CBal-1 in the Balancing Your Core Belief set. They include detailed explanations of what you can do to do to fix things permanently and how to do this. You will notice I refer to these other books in this, the main book. And there's a third pdf as well.

However they are not available yet on Kindle so I am happy to e-mail them to you ***(Free No cost)*** as pdf files.

A. Book CBal-2 "Discovering Your Unbalanced Core Belief" is a Workbook. It includes extra Activity Sheets you can use to look more closely at your F reactions. It also includes more case studies.

B. Book CBal-3 "Balancing Your Two Core Beliefs" is a hands-on script to guide you through the steps you take, either by yourself, working me John Bligh Nutting on Skype or Zoom, or with a trained Core Belief professional first to discover more about your opposite ***positive core belief*** and then balance it with your old negative one.

C. A short pdf file of each of the 20-24 Activity sheets in this book so you can print them and use them to keep a record of your survey scores and your answers to essential questions. I explained on page18 why these records are so important when you are getting ready to balance you core belief.

If you are reading this book on Amazon Kindle may I suggest you contact me and arrange for me to send you these free books by e-mail.

That includes:

A. The book files in pdf format sent by e-mail so you can print your own copies.

B. If you would like it, a **free 25- 30 minute live personal one-to-one video session** with me on Skype or Zoom or by phone, to answer questions or even take you through the actual balancing process.

I am happy to e-mail the pdf files it *at no cost* if you contact me:

bligh4@growingaware.com

...... giving me the details of the date you purchased this Core Belief book from Amazon and please tell me whether it was a Kindle copy or an actual paperback copy of the book.

If you have time, I'd also appreciate any feedback about how you are finding this book so far. Thanks,

John B Nutting

My Published Books 2020

Order now as pdf files by e-mail bligh4@growingaware.com or through my websites.
Discounts 20%-60% if you order 3 or more.
These titles will be available later this year on Amazon Kindle and as hard copies through Amazon

1. **Love Your Inner Child** set (two books)
   Code E $14.95 USD for the set
   Training edition for Profesionals Code E P
2. **Being the Real You** (four books)
   Code R $14.95 USD for the set
3. **Emotional Age Flying Awareness** set(two books)
   Code A $14.95 USD for the set
4. **Core Belief Balancing** set (four books)
   Code C-Bal $14.95 USD for the set
   Training edition for Profesionals Code C-Bal P
5. **Personal Power** set (five books) Making powerful changes, Secrets of personal power.
   Codes P and S $14.95 USD for the set
6. **Voice dialogue books** (three books)
   Code V $14.95 USD for the set
7. **Extracts from original** 1997 Growing Awareness
   Code G $14.95 USD for the set
8. **New titles** - Only in draft or being edited
   Getting Started - Best Places to begin working
   Code Q

** Emotional Age Awareness*

A-1. "Flying Awareness" (108 pages) Explains the power of Emotional Age Awareness

A-2. "Flying Higher with Emotional Age Awareness" More detailed explanations of key topics. Activity sheets.

** Growing Peace and Freedom*

G-18 "Growing Peace and Freedom - *Understanding and Ending Addictive Cycles"* includes some of the very latest information about addictive cycles, how to identify them, deal with them and how not to deal with them.

Other Book Titles

Narcissitc Behaviour Patterns (Code NBP)
Freeing Yourself from Addictive Cycles (Code G 18)
Adverse Childhood Experiences survey (Code ACE)

Short how-to-do-it notes and extracts from other books

Boundaries
Emotional Gym
Feelings are OK
Inner Parent Induction
Disowned parts of your personality
Negative Bonding patterns
$4.50 USD each sent as a pdf file or $9.90 USD for all six

** Love Your Inner Child*

E-1. "Love Your inner Child " with Personal Activity sheets, full instructions and explanations to help you get to know your Inner child, communicate with her or him every day and then discover much more about your Inner Child and the Younger Selves.

** Understanding Narcissistic Behaviour Patterns and NBP Games*

NBP-1 Do you have a partner or a close family member who regularly criticises, blames, judges you, keeps finding fault with what you do?

Does it seem nothing you can do for them is ever good enough? Do they claim they are never wrong and yet get angry if <u>you</u> try to defend yourself.

This book explains the hidden reasons behind these patterns, why they do this and powerful ways to protect yourself from their NBP Games.

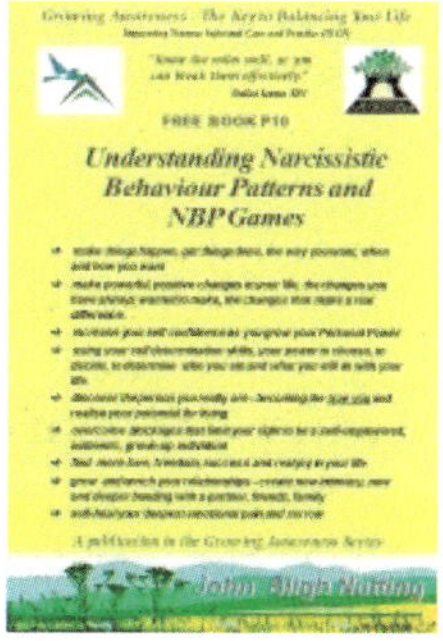

Rules for the School of Life

1. **You are enrolled in a full-time informal school called Life.** Each day you will have the opportunity to learn lessons. You may like the lessons or think them irrelevant and stupid but each one has a purpose that is special for you.

2. **A lesson will be presented to you in various forms.** It will is repeated until you have learned it. When you have learned it, you can then go on to the next lesson.

3. **Lessons may appear before you are ready,** but you will only learn a lesson when you are ready for it - If you're not ready, you will do whatever you need to do to avoid learning it - That may be how it has to be for the present. Don't worry, when you are truly ready the lesson will be presented again.

4. **There are no mistakes, only lessons.** - Growing is a process of trial and error and experimenting. The 'failed' experiments are as much a part of your learning as the experiment that ultimately 'works'.

5. **Anything that presents you with a lesson can also be a teacher.** The best lessons and the best teachers present you with the right task but not the 'right' answer. Instead they will guide you towards a number of answers and help you discover the ones that will work best for you, in the long run.

6. **Learning lessons does not end.** - There is no part of life that does not contain its lessons. If you are alive, there are lessons to be learned.

7. **"There" is no better than "here".** - When your "there" has become a "here", you will simply be presented with another "there" that will again look better than "here".

8. **Others are merely mirrors of you.** - If you love, desire, hate or reject something about another person it reflects something you love, desire, hate or reject about yourself.

9. **The answers to Life's lessons lie inside you.** All you need to do is look, listen and trust. You have all the tools and resources you need. What you do with them is up to you. What you make of your life is up to you and how you do it is your choice.

10. **You will forget all this,** until you have learned that it too is one of the lessons.

Original author unknown

Adapted from a similar list of rules, as quoted in "Chicken Soup for the Soul" by Cherie Carter-Scott

Alphabetic Index

A

B

C

D

E

F

G

H

I

J

K

Copying this publication - special permissions and Restrictions

If you are part of a Twelve step group, or an organisation that supports clients from underprivileged or low economic groups I would be happy to set up an alternate arrangement which is for me to give your group your group or organisation written authority to print or copy sections of this book at no charge.

In return I will ask for your written permission to publish a message on my websites:

- ** naming your group or organisation*
- ** acknowledging that I have donated the work to your group free of cost*
- ** feedback or stories about the ways your clients or members are benefiting by using this publication.*

This is the only situation where normal copyright restrictions do not apply.

Please contact the Publisher:

Growing Awareness Pty Ltd
bligh4@growingaware.com
PO Box 133
Bald Hills Queensland 4036
Australia

Cell / mobile +061 414 57 00 16

My websites
www.core-beliefs-balance.com
www.love-your-inner-child.com
www.voice-dialogue-inner-self-awareness.com
www.realme1.com

E-mail:
bligh4@growingaware.com

Printed in Great Britain
by Amazon

13581045R00069